An Invitation to Explore:
New International Perspectives in
Children's Literature

An Invitation to Explore: New International Perspectives in Children's Literature

Edited by:

Laura Atkins

Nolan Dalrymple

Michele Gill

Liz Thiel

Pied Piper Publishing

First published 2008 by:

Pied Piper Publishing Ltd.
80 Birmingham Road
Shenstone
Lichfield
Staffordshire
WS14 0JU

Front cover picture detail from *Udolpho the justworthy and forester of the Schwarzwald*. Available at www.bookchilde.org.

British Library Cataloguing in Publication
A catalogue record for this book is available from the British Library.

ISBN: 978 0 9552106 3 1   (10 digit - 0 9552106 3 1)

Contents

Acknowledgements

The papers selected for this volume were chosen from those presented at the third The Child and the Book PhD conference in April 2006, which was hosted by the University of Newcastle upon Tyne. The Child and the Book is an annual conference which brings together postgraduate students from all disciplines whose work is concerned with children and literature. The conference was, as always, an international event and the diversity of the delegates is reflected in the variety and breadth of the papers included in this collection. Thank you to all those who have supported, and continue to support The Child and the Book, and to the authors whose contributions have made this publication possible.

The Editors would also like to thank Peter Hunt, who kindly agreed to write the Introduction to this volume and acted as a reviewer, Elizabeth Howard, for her diligent reading, and academic reviewers Peter Bramwell, Charles Butler, Rachel Falconer, Geoff Fox, Adrienne Gavin, Mel Gibson, Matthew Grenby, Gillian Lathey, Sharyn Pierce, Pat Pinsent, Kim Reynolds, David Rudd, Karen Sands-O'Connor, Roberta Trites, Jean Webb and Christine Wilkie Stibbs.

Laura Atkins
Nolan Dalrymple
Michele Gill
Liz Thiel

Introduction: The Worldliness of Children's Literature

Peter Hunt

Professor Emeritus, Cardiff University, UK

> 'And beyond the Wild Wood again?' [Mole] asked: 'Where it's all blue and dim, and one sees what may be hills or perhaps they mayn't, and something like the smoke of towns, or is it only cloud-drift?'
>
> 'Beyond the Wild Wood comes the Wide World,' said the Rat. 'And that's something that doesn't matter, either to you or me. I've never been there, and I'm never going, nor you either, if you've got any sense at all. Don't ever refer to it again, please. Now then! Here's our backwater at last, where we're going to have lunch.' - Kenneth Grahame, *The Wind in the Willows* (1908, Chapter 1)

> 'You've only a few yards to go,' [the White Knight] said, 'down the hill and over that little brook, and then you'll be a Queen - But you'll stay and see me off first?' he added as Alice turned with an eager look in the direction to which he pointed. 'I shan't be long. You'll wait and wave your handkerchief when I get to that turn in the road? I think it'll encourage me, you see.'
>
> 'Of course I'll wait,' said Alice: 'and thank you very much for coming so far - and for the song - I liked it very much.'
>
> 'I hope so,' the Knight said doubtfully: 'but you didn't cry as much as I thought you would.' - Lewis Carroll, *Through the Looking Glass* (1871, Chapter 8)

An Invitation to Explore is an internationalist view of children's literature that ranges horizontally, as it were, from Korea to Norway, laterally from evolution to apocalypse, and vertically from individual child-reader to cultural theory. It operates confidently, as it should, upon three premises that have long since ceased to need any justification: that texts produced for children are worthy of - indeed, require and demand - serious critical and philosophical debate; that the tools and methods and theories for such a debate are in place; and that these books and these debates should not, geographically, have a privileged centre, any more than the texts should be placed on an abstract ladder of value, or the theory categorised in relation to debates on other subject-matter.

All well and very good, and a wide range of material and approach is only to be expected in the study of children's literature, which, contrary to some persistent assumptions, makes more connections and requires more skills than many disciplines. The internationalist element is an additional and tricky one, and so, as the range of subject-matter practically guarantees a diverse audience, it might be worth pausing here to consider some of the premises and paradoxes underlying both children's literature (the body of texts intended for children) and Children's Literature (the study of these texts and their contexts), and their relationship to the wide world. Initiates might move straight on to the papers.

Let us begin by venturing into the treacherous Forest of Similes.

One salutary view of children's literature - that is, the collected corpus of texts-for-children - is that it is like an airport. It is a place that you go through, and it is very exciting and thrilling and sparkling with goodies and expectations and desires and decisions, moments of high emotion that may leave their mark for life - and a steep learning curve. But it is only a place that you pass through on your way to more exciting, world-wide places. At the same time, an airport can be a deeply unlovely place, under the glitter: full of fear and strangers, and yet, for all that, it is relatively safe, temporarily secure and grounded, compared with the world outside (or what is coming next). It is not, however, a place that normal people want to stay in, although they may sometimes be glad to get back to it as a kind of relief, or, just possibly, to re-visit an emotional moment (although not many people actually want to do that). There are a few, the plane-spotters (aka the specialist literary societies), who take a deeper interest, and we might regard them as being either mildly or manically eccentric or of showing skilled and appropriate appreciation for complex human and technical achievements which the less perceptive don't appreciate. There are, of course, the workers who have to be there - the caterers, the security people, the check-in staff, the engineers (aka the writers, publishers, teachers, and scholars) who all do their best - but who are not very likely to gain great kudos for what they do. Indeed, while many airports - some airports - are architectural and sociological masterpieces, it is unlikely that they are ever going to be appreciated, in the wider world, because the fact of being airports: airports are, necessarily, inferior to most other buildings. An airport, then, like children's literature, is a curious mixture of the functional and the romantic, somewhere exciting, but somewhere where you need some very unromantic skills in order to get around. It is not a place to not concentrate, as so many adults, irritatingly, do not.

Children's literature - texts-for-children - is, in short, far more worldly-wise than the casual reader might suppose: not only does it know about the world out there (as demonstrated in this volume by Sylvia Warnecke's exploration of children's books in the GDR) but it understands - indeed, subsists in - an understanding of the relationship between the world out there and the world on the way to out there. (Which is why, if you look at the two opening quotations, you can see that *The Wind in the Willows* isn't a children's book, and *Through the Looking Glass* is!) There have been centuries of children's books whose authors have constructed certain sorts of childhood - generally 'innocent', usually vulnerable, almost invariably protected. But just because adults cast children in this role (most sinisterly, as was once famously, or infamously, pointed out by Jacqueline Rose (1984)) does not mean that children actually take on that role - any more than the child in the airport is docile, or accepts at face value the distractions or disciplines offered to it. The children rioting at the coaching inn, or sitting listening to the hell-fire tales of early children's books in Spartan schoolrooms were not, cannot have been, mere empty vessels - or only to the extent that a modern child (psychologically) chained in front of a television set is an empty vessel. The reader activates the book - activates the interaction with the author - and it is naïve to suppose that that interaction is simple and predictable. The bidden child does not miraculously change into the bidding adult. Consequently, writing about genres of children's books, at its best, takes into account potential affect as with the essays in this book by Michele Gill on the modern boys' adventure stories about Alex Rider, Cassie Hague on apocalyptic youth fiction, which uses Foucault's concepts of limit, Liz Thiel on David Almond, and Jennifer Sattaur using Jungean psychology on 'dark' fiction.

And the situation remains complex. Take the worldly-wise child postulated in children's books today. In Janet and Alan Ahlberg's apparently bucolic *The Jolly Postman* (1986) - the Big Bad Wolf receives a letter from Little Red Riding Hood's solicitors: in the Eugene Trivizas/Helen Oxenbury picture-book, *The Three Little Wolves and the Big Bad Pig* (1993), the wolves build their third house of Plexiglas and armour-plates. The point here is not that the dangers of the world have changed from mere teeth to the terrors of the law and the nightmare of the terrorist pig with the dynamite - but the continuance of the tacit acknowledgement in children's literature that the children are far from ignorant of a savage world. They are conceived by the authors as being street-smart - which means (as it has always done) that authors credit the children they create as both characters and audience with the skills necessary to survive in the world that they also posit. Terry Pratchett, is perhaps the most notable of authors who give their characters and readers such credit, as in *The Wee Free Men* (2003). Pratchett is a fierce satirist, and as with all children's writers, is colluding in serious play with the readers that he has defined: readers, as they always have (if they agree to play) take on the role, the characteristics given to them. This happens, of course, with every reading act: the big, and inescapable complication with children's books is that there are bound to be massive differences between adult writer and child reader because they are adults and children: the interaction, the play, the generation of meaning must inevitably be a complex shifting thing. (Some of the implications of this gap are explored in Noga Applebaum's essay 'A Future without a Past: Technology and History in Three Children's Science Fiction Novels'.) This is where (and not before time, possibly) the analogy with the airport breaks down: imagine a crowd of children running around the airport, jumping the adult barriers and pushing the adult buttons and testing the carefully thought-out adult systems, then we have something like children's literature.

Consequently, writers and thinkers approaching these texts, as the essays in this book demonstrate, must work in the knowledge that the field is made unstable by its paradoxes. The key words, or watchwords, are power, control, balance, and freedom, which are themselves the ingredients of understanding or domination, because of the presence of the audience, as implied or conceived in the texts, and of the involvement of real children in the literary process. As Aidan Chambers put it in 1985:

> What ten years of teaching children's literature has taught me most clearly is that, so far as children and literature are concerned, the literature itself and critical approaches to it cannot be divorced from considerations of how the literature should be mediated to children. Put another way: *Any comprehensively useful criticism of children's literature must incorporate a critical exploration of the questions raised by the problem of helping children to read the literature* [italics sic] (1985: 123)

Which brings us to the other 'Children's Literature' - the Children's Literature that appears in the titles of courses and academic books: this is the study, an autonomous world which sometimes, regrettably (and pace Chambers), operates completely independently of books and readers, rather as many religions appear to operate independently of their spiritual origins. Now, back to simile land, Children's Literature Studies can be seen as being like either (or both) Clark Kent or Linda Lee, or Ragged Dick: to take on something as inherently difficult as children's literature, it has thrown off its mild manners and become not only very powerful, but also streetwise.

Being streetwise in Academia City means being able to speak the language ('provides a ludic space for readers to escape their material positions,' 'mediates the character through the locus of control that is the text'); being able to produce the books and articles ('Dialogue and Dialectic: Language and Class in *The Wind in the Willows*'), and mastering the frequently ludicrous academic conference behaviour rituals (such as reading written text to the audience at incomprehensible speeds). On the other hand, joining the academic game also means pushing the boundaries of what can be said and thought about the books, and at its best, as in *An Invitation to Explore*, the boundaries, intellectual and geographical, are lucidly and accessibly pushed.

Looking at children's literature (or airports), then, we must be aware of these challenging (or bewildering) complexities: but Children's Literature has saddled itself with another conundrum: internationalism. Because the adjective 'children's' in 'children's literature' is of a different order from, say, 'American' as in 'American literature', the subject has taken upon itself an internationalism that is very rare in other humanities subjects (the Drama has some elements of it.). In this scenario, childhood is an international constant, providing a true basis for comparative literary studies, and, even more optimistically, a beacon for future international understanding. But such romantic, not to say sentimental, attitudes are hardly tenable, and, as Emer O'Sullivan has pointed out, were encouraged by the French enthusiast for children's literature, Paul Hasard. The most influential part of Hasard's legacy was

> his vision of the 'universal republic of childhood' which knows no ... borders and no foreign languages; in it, the children of all nations read the children's books of all nations: 'Smilingly the pleasant books of childhood cross all the frontiers; there is no duty to be paid on inspiration' (Hazard, 1932/1944: 147). Children's books, ambassadors of their countries, transcend borders with ease and forge bonds between all the children of the world: 'Every country gives and every country receives.' This is an idealistic way of talking about children's literature which ignores both the conditions that determine its production and those which influence its transfer between countries (O'Sullivan, 2004: I; 14)

It certainly ignores the imbalance of translations - the tiny proportions of translations into English, as compared to translations from English (Hunt, 2000: 107-112) - let alone an embarrassing Anglocentrism. Take Alison Lurie, in *Boys and Girls Forever* (2003) where she says, unblushingly,

It is interesting to note that ... perhaps the majority [of famous writers for children] are British or American, just as so many of the best-loved children's books are British or American. Other nations have produced a single brilliant classic or series: Denmark, for instance, has Andersen's tales; Italy has Pinocchio, France has Babar, Finland has Moomintroll. A list of famous children's books in English, however, could easily take up a page... (Lurie, 2003: x)

Fortunately, that is not a view shared by the remarkable number of polyglot scholars of and enthusiasts for children's texts worldwide (witness the strength of IBBY, the International Board on Books for Young Readers, with its more than 70 branches, from - a salutary fact for the Anglophiles - Rwanda to Kazakhstan). In the present book, the essays by Sarah Park on Korean, Farsad Boobani on Iranian, and Åse Marie Ommundsen on Norwegian children's literature, provide a corrective to this kind of attitude.

Nevertheless, there is a commercial and cultural pressure towards localisation or 'domestication' of texts, on the assumption (which is ludicrously flattering to adults) that 'Young readers cannot be expected to have acquired the breadth of understanding of other cultures, languages and geographies that are taken for granted in an adult readership' (Lathey, 2006: 7).

But we should try, and international conferences in children's literature, for all their imperfections, and for all the honest doubts that an observer might have about quite what is being understood, seem to me to be entirely admirable. After all, what constitutes valuable, measurable, understanding, when the normal gulf between addresser and addressee in our subject and our subject matter is by definition so wide? One of the many surreal aspects of modern travel is this very question of international communication, or lack of it. Thus it came as rather a shock to me to realise, walking through Osaka airport (once), that there were signs in English everywhere - which can easily mislead the unwary into thinking that you actually understand something about the place where you are. Equally, I always feel curiously cheered when English isn't there: when, say, the pilot on a flight from Oslo to Tromsø doesn't feel the need to make announcements in anything but Norwegian. That brings home the fact that (especially if you are a monoglot Englishperson) you really are in a different world, where things are done differently. Either we think we understand what to do - or what books are 'about' - because things are made 'the same' through being Englished, or we move along, as in a fog - or, perhaps, a bright light - either not seeing properly, or seeing something that we have not seen before.

Internationalism, in children's books as in airports, is something to be welcomed, but not to be domesticated, and, as the essays in this book demonstrate it is rare that topics can be confined to one culture or one genre. Thus Alison Pipitone considers the influence of the very British Antony Hope's *The Prisoner Of Zenda* on the boy who became the 32nd President of the USA; Ulf Schöne's exploration of anarchism in children's literature uses British, German, and Swedish examples; Laura Atkins and Anastasia Economidou discuss the way that picturebooks are read, using close readings of Japanese and Greek texts, respectively.

One collection of essays, one meeting of minds covering everything from picture books, manga, science fiction, apocalyptic fiction, war, boys' fiction, and myth, to Jung, anarchy, evolution (Zoe Jaques on Darwin and Kingsley) and, constantly, social history and affect. Overall, an invitation to explore that also invites us to leave behind our prejudices, embrace the new, and be grateful for the skills and open-mindedness of our guides, as all good travellers should.

Bibliography

Ahlberg, Janet and Alan (1986) *The Jolly Postman*. London: Penguin.

Chambers, Aidan (1985) *Booktalk*. London: Bodley Head

Hazard, Paul (1932/1944) *Books, Children and Men*. Mitchell, M (trans.) Boston: The Horn Book

Hunt, Peter (2000) Children's Literature, in France, Peter (ed.) *The Oxford Guide to Literature in English Translation*. Oxford: Oxford University Press

Lathey, Gillian (ed.) (2006) *The Translation of Children's Literature. A Reader*. Clevedon, Buffalo, Toronto: Multilingual Matters

Lurie, Alison (2003) *Boys and Girls Forever*, London: Chatto and Windus

O'Sullivan, Emer (2004) Internationalism and the Universal Child, in Hunt, Peter (ed) *International Companion Encyclopedia of Children's Literature*. 2nd Edn, London and New York, Routledge I, 13-25

Rose, Jacqueline (1984) *The Case of Peter Pan, or the Impossibility of Children's Fiction*. Basingstoke: Macmillan

Trivizas, Eugene (illust. Oxenbury, Helen) (1993) *The Three Little Wolves and the Big Bad Pig*. London: Heinemann

A Future without a Past: Technology and History in Three Children's Science Fiction Novels

Noga Applebaum

What does science fiction for the young have to say about the impact of technology on history? How do adults choose to address the technological gap between themselves and children in view of its potential to undermine their own authority? The three novels analysed associate the past with positive human values - what defines us as human. Technology is associated with the future; it is seen as a potentially dehumanising force. This anti-technological bias not only undermines the sense of wonder intrinsic to SF, but is alarming if we consider the fact that young people are often more comfortable with new technologies than their teachers and parents.

In the first of a recent series of the Reith lectures, entitled The Triumph of Technology, Lord Broers, a leading engineer, stated that 'the possession of an understanding of technology, just as with an understanding of music, literature, or the arts, brings with it great personal satisfaction and pleasure' (Broers, 2005). It is not a coincidence that Lord Broers chose to link technology and the arts in his passionate manifesto calling for better public appreciation for the contribution of technology to human culture. Underlying his statement is an acknowledgment that a rift may exist between the sciences and the humanities, as well as an attempt to bridge it by drawing positive parallels between these fields of human endeavour.

The divide implied by Lord Broers's statement was overtly critiqued in C P Snow's renowned 1959 Rede lecture, entitled 'The Two Cultures'. Snow, himself a scientist by training and a novelist by practice, lamented what he claimed was a widening gap between the sciences and the humanities as a result of specialisation within the British education system (Snow and Collini, 1993). Snow observed that between literary intellectuals and scientists lies 'a gulf of mutual incomprehension - sometimes (particularly among the young) hostility and dislike, but most of all lack of understanding. They have a curious distorted image of each other' (Snow and Collini, 1993: 4). His lecture sparked a controversy[1] as scholars from both sides of the debate argued over Snow's conclusions that indeed two cultures exist, and that scientists have 'the future in their bones' while humanities' scholars are 'natural Luddites' (Snow and Collini, 1993: 10, 22). Spearheading the attack on Snow was F R Leavis, a prominent literary critic who spared no words to convey his contempt for Snow, whom he saw as speaking for that which reduces 'human experience to the quantifiable, the measurable, the manageable' (Snow and Collini, 1993: xxxiii). The controversy carried on for decades beyond Snow's and Leavis's own time.

This debate exemplifies the extent to which modern scholars have tried to negotiate the roles of the humanities and the sciences in a rapidly changing world.[2] Scholars generally do not deny that culture has altered as a result of technological advances; however, opinions do vary as to the moral nature of this alteration and its impact on what is considered human. In fact, the essential definition of what it is that defines our humanity is under investigation in this debate. Both sides equate humanity with creativity and morality. The discussion is, therefore, between those who oppose technology on the grounds that it dehumanises people, alienates them from each other and themselves, and produces or accompanies manipulative ideology, and those who champion technology's ability to bring culture to the masses, create new means for artistic expression as well as provide a better life for people, allowing them more leisure time to pursue the arts. Another element in the debate is which direction society should face in order to preserve its sense of humanity - whether it is backwards into the past, represented by the already accrued wisdom of philosophy, arts and religion, or forward into the future, as Kranzberg suggests, 'redefining old values and creating new ones more in keeping with our technological and democratic civilization' (Kranzberg, 1979: 173).

Science fiction may be seen as a meeting point between 'science' and 'art,' as the genre's name suggests. As Brian Stableford points out in the *Encyclopedia of Science Fiction*, science fiction (SF) authors, themselves artists after all, often argue that 'the emotional richness of art is necessary to temper and redeem the cold objectivity of science.' Nevertheless, one of the trademarks of adult SF as a genre is the authors' intrinsic belief that 'technological progress is the principal facilitator of moral progress' (Clute and Nicholls, 1999: 53, 1202). In this sense, technology is often depicted in genre SF as a source of wonder, and is celebrated as another aspect of human creativity.

However, the strong association of children's literature with education (Campbell, 2003: 34), and the growing public concern regarding the decline of young people's book reading habits in the face of the mounting competition over their leisure time by technological pastimes such as computer games and the internet, may well have an impact on the way children's SF authors choose to depict the role of the humanities in a technologised future. Another crucial phenomenon which may affect children's SF authors' attitudes towards technology is the generational know-how gap, as surveys point to a common adult fear that 'the emerging competence divide between the ICT skills of some parents/teachers and their children threatens to puncture their identity, status and authority as adults' (Valentine and Holloway, 2001: 67).

In this essay, I will focus on the field of history, attempting to unearth the underlying attitudes towards the impact of technology on history in three SF novels in which the relationship between past and future is explored. Through the authors' representations of scientists and historians within the narrative, as well as their depiction of the fate of the past in a technological environment, I will investigate the range of perspectives on offer in these texts and by extension the value systems promoted within them. This investigation may offer some insight as to how adults choose to address the technological gap between themselves and children in view of its potential to undermine their own authority.

History - past - memory

'The past...It's gone, lost. History drowned and we pulled up the ladder behind us' says Dr Rémy Turcat, the archaeologist in Jan Mark's *Useful Idiots* (2004: 18). This statement represents the state of affairs not only in *Useful Idiots*, but in two other children's SF novels: *The Giver* (Lowry, 1993) and *Mortal Engines* (Reeve, 2001).

The futuristic societies described in the three novels are detached from their past. In two of the books this detachment begins as a result of a technological disaster. In *Mortal Engines*, the Sixty Minute War brought on the destruction of advanced civilisation as well as the devastation of the planet by powerful technological weapons (p7), while in *Useful Idiots* a sophisticated computer virus has wiped out the records of the new Pan-European state to which the half-drowned British Isles belong (p16). The implication is, therefore, that technology poses a threat to history. In Mark's book, the use of artificial memory, in the form of computerised archives, is not seen as liberating, 'freeing the mind to pursue other goals' (Murphie and Potts, 2003: 159), but rather as a dangerous dependency.

In all three books, the technological and post-technological societies, especially their governing bodies, choose to remain detached from certain parts of their history. In *Useful Idiots*, archaeology is the rediscovered 'lost science' (p10)[3], confined to the local university together with history, 'an undersubscribed specialism' (p72). However, archaeology, 'in the view of the general public could remain lost' (pp10-11). Having genetically improved the quality of life and its length, the new society closed the museums, which served as constant reminders that 'life might be prolonged indefinitely but no one had yet come up with a way to make it infinite' (p11). In Mark's novel, advanced technology offers people a healthier, better future; however, this leaves them less equipped to deal with their own mortality, for centuries considered a fundamental part of being a human being, and as a result the preoccupation of history and archaeology with death is considered primitive and is viewed with 'disgust' (p71). Therefore, it is not only the unreliability of technology as means to store human history which Mark alerts us to, but also that living in an advanced technological environment could cause society to become less interested in its own history.

A further objection to researching the past in *Useful Idiots* is fear that it would give rise to racialism and nationalism. The government views the past as a potential threat since indigenous culture and a shared history may serve as weapons in undermining the homogeneity and Pan-European identity they strive to construct. The futuristic community described in *The Giver* has also faced the fear of diversity and difference leading to conflict and pain, and has chosen an extreme solution. The Elders of the community have passed on all responsibility for long-term memory, in both the collective and the individual sense, to one person, entitled the Receiver; and for generations the community has no recollection of their own history. The Receiver is not a machine, but flesh and blood; however, the act of relinquishing the responsibility to remember by transferring large quantities of historical data from one's own mind to another receptacle is similar to saving records on a computer, and thus from the point of view of the community the Receiver can be perceived as synonymous with artificial memory. Therefore, the disastrous consequences of relying on an outside source to retain history which unravel in the novel can be seen as a metaphor for the dependency on technological archives and implies that Lowry shares Mark's views regarding the threat that technology poses for humans' interest in and knowledge of history. The fact that the Elders of the community use technologies such as monitoring devices, mind-altering drugs and genetic engineering to keep the community in check, reinforces this assumption, as the author continually posits technology as an accomplice in the dehumanising process that the community goes through from the point in time when they chose to disengage with their past.

Furthermore, in *The Giver*, Lowry seems to make no distinction between collective history and personal memory. Jonas, the trainee, is exposed to individual memories such as a sledge ride in the snow or a specific family's Christmas celebration, as well as to historical collective events, such as war and famine. The fact that individual memories and collective history are presented as synonymous concepts within the novel emphasises the link that Lowry asserts between history and human identity. The novel suggests that our personal memory shapes us as human beings, as it provides us with the context which is vital for experiencing emotions such as love or anger in their full depths. In the same manner, collective history is the essence of humanity, without which society is bound to dehumanise. The relinquishing of collective history is as traumatic to the human race as is the loss of memory to an individual.

While Lowry's novel depicts a whole society detached from its memory, Mark's and Reeve's novels portray subgroups resisting the move away from history. The aboriginals in *Useful Idiots*, known by the derogatory nickname Oysters, strive to keep their national identity by holding fast to old customs and traditions while living in designated enclosed reserves. Part of the aboriginals' struggle to preserve their history includes a refusal to be genetically modified, even at a price of disease and early death. It is not only their physical appearance which distinguishes them from the society around them. They also dwell in cottages, maintain close familial relationships, and elect to live without surveillance to the astonishment of Merrick Korda, the European archaeology student.[4] In contrast, he lives, as all Europeans do, on his own, in newly built tower blocks which one cannot enter without passing through an electronic recognition system (Mark, 2004: 156). Frida, the aboriginal dancer, remarks that unlike the Europeans whose surveillance systems collect preposterous amounts of useless information, her people 'choose what to record of ourselves' (p158). Mark ironically implies that a technologically advanced society is so obsessed with collecting superficial physical information through devices such as CCTV and retinal scans, that it becomes detached from its humanity and neglects to preserve the information that really matters, its historical and cultural heritage.

However, the apparent gap between the aboriginal and European societies' attitudes towards the past and the preservation of culture is suddenly narrowed by the end of Mark's novel. The aboriginals were granted their special status after it was found that greedy Europeans had taken advantage of their unmodified immune systems to infect them with a disease causing the growth of valuable 'pearls' in human joints, only to harvest their bodies after death (hence the pejorative name 'Oysters'). A few generations later these crimes were forgotten and the aboriginals' status became threatened again as part of the state's campaign to uproot nationalism, the same campaign which closed down the archaeology department at the university. Korda, determined to remind the state of the past, infects himself with the disease, intending to use the 'pearl' in court as evidence, but he is betrayed by the very people he set out to help as he seeks refuge in the reserve. He is abducted by the locals and his pearl is stolen from him. Korda leaves the reserve with nothing more than a bitter realisation that the aboriginals were 'no more high-minded than any other Europeans' (p395), and that he was the only one interested in the truth (p407). The truth in this case is synonymous with history, and the aboriginals' betrayal signifies a change in their attitude towards the past. This change may well be attributed to the influence of the society around them. This influence is made possible via technology, as the aboriginals, to Korda's surprise, have installed screens in their homes (p159) and use telecommunication ear studs (p164). Ed, the aboriginal mayor of the reserve comments that the younger aboriginals are 'quite desperate to get away' (p259), to assimilate, as Korda's own ancestors have done, losing interest in their national identity (p241). Technology, therefore, assists in the disintegration of indigenous cultures.[5] In this sense, the ending of the book implies that society's dismissal of history results in the slow decline of human values such as friendship and trust which will leave people lonely and detached from their own community, as Korda finds himself at the close of the novel.

It is important to note that while the Europeans and the aboriginals are depicted as untrustworthy, and their motivations sinister, the academics featured in the book seem to have a genuine interest in the past. Although the archaeologist Turcat fleetingly considers the idea of selling the pearls he found to fund more research, he redeems himself by trying to assist Korda in preparing the court case (p396). Korda himself, persistently fighting for truth and knowledge to the extent of self-sacrifice, is the embodiment of the humane academic, the keeper of truth, whose blazing idealism and childlike naiveté leave him vulnerable, a 'useful idiot' in the hands of corrupt politicians and greedy opportunists (ibid.). Ed ironically refers to Korda as 'the man who saved the past' (p167). Korda's failure to do just that, despite his good intentions, suggests that Mark foresees a grim fate for the humanities in a technological age.

An even more powerful literary manifestation of C P Snow's concept of the split between the scientists and the humanists, is found in Reeve's *Mortal Engines*. The traction city of London is divided into guilds; the two prestigious ones are the guild of Historians who are based in the Museum of London, and the guild of Engineers, who ensure the smooth running of the city. Reeve contrasts the guilds in both appearance and attitude and highlights their rivalry.

The Historians, to which Tom, the young protagonist belongs, firmly believe that 'history was just as important as bricks and iron and coal' (Reeve, 2001: 14), and that they 'create knowledge' without which the other guilds would not be able to function as efficiently (ibid.). For the Historians, therefore, the past always underpins the present and society must be looking 'backwards into time,' as their guild mark, the blue eye, symbolises (p17). By contrast, the members of the Guild of Engineers openly declare that they 'are the future' (p255), and their only interest in the past is Old-Tech, scraps from the civilisation which destroyed itself in the Sixty Minute War (p201). The Historians make a distinction between ancient artefacts such as bones, paintings and books, all considered historically valuable, and old technology which is not perceived as a creative human endeavour and therefore does not share this prestigious status.

The Engineers, on the other hand, have no qualms about burning the Museum's art collections when more fuel is needed to feed the furnaces and keep the city's fast pace (ibid.). Moreover, they choose to launch MEDUSA, a weapon capable of destroying whole civilisations, from St. Paul's cathedral, a potent symbol of history, art and religion. The engineers are scientists, but they are interested purely in destructive science and technology, building weapons and cyborgs for colonial purposes. The Historians, on the other hand, 'had never been as quick as the rest of London to welcome new inventions' (p199). Thus Reeve makes a hierarchical distinction between the humanists who seek to preserve culture and the scientists who seek to destroy it.

This distinction is further emphasised by the appearance and value system of the two guilds. Members of the Historians guild are depicted as musty, eccentric academics, devoted to their fields of speciality and stereotypically keen tea and biscuit consumers. However, they are also portrayed as 'kind' (p200). Although they confess to having 'no idea how to stand up to the Guild of Engineers' (p202), they are nevertheless determined to stop MEDUSA and show exceptional courage in doing so (pp256-257). Throughout the book the Historians, Tom included, display qualities such as loyalty, friendship, selflessness, courage and care for human lives. When Tom kills a cyborg in self-defence, he is guilt stricken (p193). His remorse stands in sharp contrast to Dr Vambrace, the Engineers' security chief who 'is always keen to find new and inventive ways to kill people' (p198). The Engineers with their white rubber robes, permanently shaved heads and rules against touching each other (p173) display cruelty, disregard for human life, blind ambition, and a detachment from their own emotions. This twisted system of values leads eventually to the destruction of London and the annihilation of its citizens. Thus Reeve not only depicts humanists and scientists as two rival cultures who fail to communicate with each other, as suggested by C.P. Snow, but very clearly posits technology and those who develop it as a dehumanising force working against the best interests of civilisation. Reeve implies, therefore, that humanity's gaze must be directed into the past, the realm of the humanities, rather than into the future which he associates with technology and the sciences.[6]

The three novels analysed in this paper share a bias against technology on the grounds that it poses a threat to human history. The past in these novels is associated with positive human values. Moreover, it is perceived as an integral component in what defines us as human. Technology is associated with the future, and by extension is presented as a potentially dehumanising force. In relation to Snow's concept of two cultures, these novels reassert that the humanities and the sciences, the latter often synonymous with technological progress, are indeed rival perspectives on the direction which humanity needs to take in the future. The authors represent the humanities, in this instance, history, in a favourable light, giving the distinct impression that they feel uneasy with technology. This anti-technological bias is alarming if we consider the fact that young people are often more comfortable with new technologies than their teachers and parents. The negative attitudes found in the novels analysed may therefore be seen as reflecting a growing anxiety within society, that the existing power balance between adults and children may be overturned by the younger generation's rapidly increasing technological mastery. The sense of wonder intrinsic to SF as a genre is undermined in these novels as the young readers are offered the superiority of the past over an innovative technological future, a future into which they are already taking their first steps.

Notes

1. Described in Collini's introduction to Snow's text.

2. See for example Ellul (1964), Steiner (1984), Smith (1996) and Russo (1998).

3. It is interesting to note that Mark refers to archaeology as a 'science', however, as an academic subject it is studied in British universities within faculties of Art, rather than Science.

4. It is important to note that the aboriginals live within a treacherous and wild natural terrain and know how to survive and navigate through it instinctively. Their abuse by the technological society emphasises that innocence is not only mythically linked to nature, but also to the past.

5. While colonial history and the 'McDonald' culture invasion prove that this point is a valid one, it is nevertheless important to note the valuable role of the internet in preserving the heritage of indigenous communities. See for example http://www.aboriginalhunter.com/, or http://www.nativeweb.org/.

6. Reeve, speaking at the IBBY-UK conference 2006, admitted that in the sequels to *Mortal Engines*, he made a conscious effort to rectify the blatant dichotomy between the historians and the engineers. Indeed in the last volume, *A Darkling Plain* (2006), the surviving historians and engineers collaborate to rebuild London as a peaceful hovering city.

Bibliography

Broers, A. (2005) *The Triumph of Technology: Reith Lectures 2005*. London, BBC.

Campbell, A. (2003) *From Looking Glass to Spyglass: A Consultation Paper on Children's Literature*. London, Arts Council England.

Clute, J. & Nicholls, P. (1999) *The Encyclopedia of Science Fiction.* London, Orbit.

Ellul, J. (1964) *The Technological Society.* New York, Vintage.

Kranzberg, M. (1979) Technology the Civilizer. *Iowa State Journal of Research.* 54, pp163-173.

Lowry, L. (1993) *The Giver.* London, Collins

Murphie, A. & Potts, J. (2003) *Culture and Technology.* Basingstoke and NY, Palgrave.

Reeve, P. (2001) *Mortal Engines.* London, Scholastic.

Reeve, P. (2006) *A Darkling Plain.* London, Scholastic.

Russo, J. P. (1998) The Humanities in a Technological Society. *Humanitas.* XI, pp14-41.

Smith, A. (1996) *Software for the Self: Culture and Technology.* London, Faber and Faber.

Snow, C. P. & Collini, S. (1993) *The Two Cultures and the Scientific Revolution.* Cambridge, Cambridge University Press.

Steiner, G. (1984) 'Future Literacies'. *George Steiner: A Reader.* Oxford, OUP.

Valentine, G. & Holloway, S. (2001) 'Technophobia': Parents and Children's Fears About Information and Communication Technologies and the Transformation of Culture and Society. In Hutchby, I. & Moran-Ellis, J. (Eds.) *Children, Technology and Culture: The Impacts of Technologies in Children's Everyday Lives.* London and New York, RoutledgeFalmer.

The research for this paper was enabled by a Doctoral Award from the Arts and Humanities Research Council. I would like to thank the AHRC for their support.

Graphic Images: Depicting the Bombing of Hiroshima in the Graphic Novel *Barefoot Gen*

Laura Atkins

Comics can show personal history in relation to major historical events in unique and exciting ways. Narrative techniques, memory and narrative authority are the keys to why a book like this might have been published for children: the comic format moves easily from individual to collective experience, and makes a strong ideological point.

Representing personal history in relationship to greater historical events offers a complex situation which I believe comics have the capacity to depict in unique and exciting ways. This area of research arose from my growing interest in the comic format, which provides a fascinating and complex juxtaposition of word and image. Scott McCloud's *Understanding Comics* (1994) provided me with particularly useful analysis of the comic format, and much of his theory underpins my investigation. This essay centres on *Barefoot Gen* (1989, 1990, 1995, 2005) by Keiji Nakazawa and aims to provide insight into this comic's ability to represent such complex and multi-layered narratives that treat the themes of history and memory; particularly in terms of a violent and disturbing event - the bombing of Hiroshima - that some might deem 'unrepresentable' for children. I will focus, in particular, on how the representation of history is juxtaposed with the personal experience and memory of the author, examining how the historical and autobiographical modes relate and how they are conveyed to the reader; looking at who narrates the story and how that relates to memory and narrative authority; and finally, addressing why a book like this might have been published for children, and with what intent.

The word manga was coined by the Japanese artist Hokusai in 1814, and can mean a caricature, cartoon, comic strip, or comic book. (Schodt, 1983: 18). A basic difference from Western comics is that manga is read from (what we perceive to be) back to front and right to left, as the Japanese language is read. These differences can make translation into English challenging. The other major difference is length, as manga tends to be much longer. Within this format, there is more attention paid to storytelling and character development, and manga generally uses fewer words and more frames and pages to show an action or thought, all of which make it possible to read manga much more quickly than Western comics. Manga is enormously popular in Japan, covering a huge number of subjects and themes, and is read by adults as well as children. Schodt notes, 'According to the Research Institute for Publications, of all the books and magazines actually sold in Japan ... manga comprised nearly *40 percent* of the total' (Schodt, 1983: 29).

The manga *Barefoot Gen* by Keiji Nakazawa chronicles the life of a boy, Gen, and his family in wartime Japan. In its English published form, there are four volumes. The first volume depicts the family's life before the bombing, and their suffering as a result of Gen's father's anti-war sentiments. It culminates with the dropping of the bomb on Hiroshima, the deaths of Gen's father and two siblings, and his mother giving birth to a baby girl. The second volume depicts the horrors of life immediately after the bomb. Gen fights hard to find food for his family, and helps other survivors as he navigates the hellish landscape of decimated Hiroshima. The third volume chronicles the family's attempt to find a place to live after the immediate impact of the bombing. They suffer rejection and humiliation as those outside of Hiroshima turn their backs on the bomb victims. Gen's spirit is central to the story as he helps a despairing victim to regain hope, and earns money to support his family. Volume four continues nine days after the bomb and shows the continuing suffering and struggle of Gen and his mother. Gen's indomitable spirit is at the heart of all four volumes.

The author, Keiji Nakazawa, was seven when the bomb dropped on Hiroshima. He lost his father, brother and sister, as does Gen in the first volume. At the age of 33, he published an autobiographical comic book account of surviving the bomb called 'I Saw It' in a Japanese children's weekly magazine. A year later, he began the fictionalised *Barefoot Gen* series in *Shukan Shonen Jampu*, the largest weekly comic magazine in Japan with a circulation of over two million ('About *Barefoot Gen*' in Nakazawa, 1990: xv). The serial ran from 1972-1973. Barbara Reynolds, in her foreword to the first and second volumes, explains why Nakazawa wrote this book for children:

> Nakazawa was distressed to find that twenty years after the war most students knew nothing about the atomic bombs and that many teachers were not sure how to teach their students about such subjects since they themselves had no experience of war (1990: v & 1999: iii)

Barefoot Gen was the first manga ever to be published in English, which was a result of the work of Project Gen, formed in 1976 by a group of Japanese and American volunteers. Their goal was to spread *Barefoot Gen's* anti-war message, and to publish it in as many languages as possible. The first volume was published in English in Tokyo in 1978, and 5000 copies were printed and distributed around the world. The second volume was published in 1979, and *Gen* was ultimately translated into over ten languages. While the books were well received by critics, they were not a commercial success. However, Last Gasp comics has recently republished all four volumes. It was also adapted as an animated movie, released in 1983.

Gen is a fictionalised character created by Nakazawa, and the name means 'roots' or 'source'. Nakazawa has said that he invented Gen as an inspiration for himself and others:

> I named my main character Gen in the hope that he would become a root or source of strength for a new generation of mankind - one that can tread the charred soil of Hiroshima barefoot, feel the earth beneath its feet, and have the strength to say 'no' to nuclear weapons.... I myself would like to live with Gen's strength - that is my ideal, and I will continue pursuing it through my work. (from 'About *Barefoot Gen*' in Nakazawa, 1990: xv)

To better understand the ways in which this memory-based book depicts history, it is important to look at who tells the story, so to examine the role of the narrator and of the implied author. In *Barefoot Gen*, Nakazawa has created a book based on his experiences, but featuring a fictionalised character. There is no first person-teller in this book, no voice of an individualised narrator. Rather, the narrator is omniscient, and the voice in the captions, as opposed to speech in speech bubbles, is primarily historical, explaining what has happened or what is happening. This essentially removes the sense of a personal telling, that the voice behind the book experienced the events in the story.

Why would Nakazawa choose to fictionalise this story? While it is impossible to know his full motives, one can posit various theories. Gillian Lathey writes about possible motives in her book on autobiographical children's literature set around World War II:

> When a traumatic *childhood* memory is the focus of an autobiographical piece, the drive to recount it may be tempered by the conflict between what has possibly been regarded as 'untellable' and the form in which it might be told. Past experience associated with pain or guilt has to be shaped into an account or a narrative to be addressed to children. Fictionalisation is a possible approach, to be followed by a more direct account of the past. (Lathey, 1998: 54)

Describing the bombing of Hiroshima, especially for children, does stand on the verge of being untellable. Nakazawa has stated that he created Gen as an inspiration, both to others and to himself; a moral actor in an incomprehensible time. The creation of a role model character allows the author to give some shape and motive to the telling, and takes Nakazawa out of the story as an actor or agent. As Barbara Reynolds writes, 'Nakazawa did not begin the task of writing *Barefoot Gen* for his own pleasure. Every memory was painful and he wanted only to forget' (Reynolds 1990: v & 1999: iii). Perhaps creating a fictionalised character allowed Nakazawa to remember in detail without fully putting himself into the story, offering him a way to distance himself from the immediacy of those horrible memories.

Because his voice is not an overt part of the telling, the role of the implied author in this book is more distant than it would be in a directly autobiographical narrative. This diminishes the authority that would come from telling a directly memory-based tale. If *Barefoot Gen* does not rely on the authority of the implied author's direct relationship to the telling, how does the telling happen and where does the narrative authority lie?

The voice of the narrator plays a key role in the *Barefoot Gen* books. These books use few captions, the place in which the textual voice of the narrator exists in the comic format. Words like 'meanwhile' are used sparingly, mostly because Gen is the almost constant focaliser so the narrative rarely needs to shift. The primary role played by the narrator in the *Barefoot Gen* books is to give historical information; to tell the reader something that Gen and the other characters do not know. For example, at the beginning of the second volume, there is a series of panels that explains what happened between the US and the Japanese governments after the bombing of Hiroshima, including the second bomb that was dropped on Nagasaki (Figure 1). The narrator says 'Knowing that Japan had no intention of surrendering unconditionally, America dropped another atomic bomb called "Fat Boy" on Nagasaki 3 days later - 11:05 a.m. August 9th' (1990: 5). The narrator gives exact times and dates, knowledge that comes in the light of history, *after* the events that are being described. This is specific information, lending the feel of historical accuracy to the story, that it is true and describes real events. Because the narrator is third person and omniscient, the voice of the narrator has the effect of being all-knowing. Thus two panels later, when the narrator says, 'As it always is when war is waged by an all-powerful dictator, those who die are the nameless and defenceless' (5), this judgmental comment is rendered as fact.

Figure 1

The narrator clearly has a position in relation to the story being told, and is critical of Japan and the Japanese government during World War II. This is not an objective representation of history, but is it possible to tell a story like this objectively? All books carry ideology, including those that represent history. John Stephens says regarding the writing of historical fiction,

> The idea of "telling it how it was" tends to implicitly mask more complex issues such as the retrospective construction of causality and the impossibility of creating narrative without a point of view. (Stephens, 1992: 202)

In this case the narrator does have a point of view, and the ideology is close to the surface and thinly masked.

This historical voice, which has knowledge of what happens after the bombing, does more than reflect back on the actions being depicted in the panel. Through knowledge of the future, the narrator sometimes creates a sense of double meaning in scenes featuring the protagonists who lack this knowledge. For instance, Gen meets a girl, Natsue, who dreamed of becoming a dancer, but has discovered that she is disfigured because of the bomb. Gen tries to protect her from this knowledge, and stops her from killing herself twice. He finally convinces her to stay alive. The final panel (Figure 2) shows Natsue from the front, winking, and Gen behind her with his fist in the air; there is a feeling of success and optimism. The voice of the narrator, however, tells a different story:

> Natsue had found the will to live, but was she really better off surviving? ... Hers would be a life of suffering with a burned face, treating keloids [disfiguring scar tissue] that would result in permanent disfigurement.... (1990: 103)

Figure 2

The words of the narrator offset Gen's hopefulness, as the narrator knows of the suffering still to come for the survivors. The visual communicates both the optimism and the dark future as both characters are smiling, but Natsue's face is shown to be covered with disfiguring scars, something which the readers may notice anew in light of the narrator's words. The pessimism of the historical voice here counters Gen's constant optimism, and creates a dual perspective within the book.

This dual narrative relates to the concept of counterpoint as described by Philip Pullman. Counterpoint is the ability for comics to show different things happening at the same time. Pullman writes:

> In a comic strip we can see several things happening together, and it doesn't matter which we read first. In the frame of the comic strip, the stream of time breaks up into little local eddies—and this loosening of the tyranny of the one-way flow makes counterpoint possible; releasing the most extraordinary virtuosity in storytelling. (Pullman, 1989: 172)

While Pullman is generally referring to the visual depiction of simultaneous stories in comics, this term can also relate to the narrative voice and its relationship to what is happening within the panel. In this case, the reader is simultaneously immersed in Gen's sense of success and optimism, and the narrator's conveyance of what Natsue's life will be like in the future. Two stories are being told simultaneously, and the visual depiction brings them together.

The narrator in the *Gen* books plays a variety of roles, as I have shown, and the implied author is disguised behind the narrator, selecting which events to show, creating Gen as an optimistic character, and providing the words and point of view that are conveyed by the narrator. So while this book lacks the implied 'truth' conveyed through an autobiographical perspective, the use of the narrative voice constructs its own authoritative telling.

While *Barefoot Gen* is focalised primarily through the lives of Gen and his family, the story is based around an historic event, one that affected masses of people. While I have looked at the role of the narrator to convey historic information, I now want to look further at the ways in which the connection is made between Gen's story and the larger historic implications of the bombing of Hiroshima, particularly using the visual format of the graphic novel.

This book treats large-scale historical events through an individual story. This creates a complex narrative which asks the reader to identify with a few stories, and to simultaneously project that identification to huge numbers of people. How does *Barefoot Gen* help the reader to make this transition? On a basic level, by telling the story of Gen and his mother, this book shows the reader the perspective of a child and a woman, two especially powerless figures. This is not the story of the leader of Japan, nor of those making the important historic decisions. It is, instead, the story of the common person, which allows for easy identification on the part of the reader. Also, the use of the simplified comic format in which characters are represented with little detail or individuation helps the reader to immerse him or herself in that character's experience (as McCloud shows in *Understanding Comics*, 1994).

Figure 3

The book also uses some textual and visual methods to enable the reader to identify first with the individual, and then make the leap from the individual story to mass experience. A place where this can be seen comes at the beginning of the second volume when Gen and his mother are starting to understand the level of destruction and death that surrounds them (Figure 3). A girl with melting skin approaches them both, says her name, and asks them to tell her parents that she died there. She then dies at their feet and Gen's mother asks Gen to 'please bury her' (1990: 2). These panels have been close-ups on the girl, Gen and his mother, and the reader has been asked to empathise with this girl's plight through the focalisation of Gen and his mother. The next panel pulls back, looking down from above and a distance, to show the large number of people who are sick and dying around them. The story has moved from one girl with a name and parents, to the large numbers like her, and the reader is asked to continue to identify with these masses as individuals through the combined depiction of text and image. This is just one example in which the book, through Gen's focalisation, depicts one person's story as a way to represent the experiences of many. The visual comic format provides an ease in moving the depiction from individual to collective.

The fact that this book is set during an historical event that is horrifying and which affected the lives of so many people, creates a unique situation in terms of reader identification. Hamida Bosmajian writes about reader identification and historical trauma in her essay, 'Nightmares of History: The Outer Limits of Children's Literature':

> Historical trauma is a collective inundation of a culture; it affects the life, not just of the individual or the small group, but of the entire social order, its past, present and future. The reader of literature about such traumas can no longer comfortably apply us/them dichotomies, for this literature universalises moral problems, choices, and consequences. (Bosmajian, 1983: 20)

According to this statement, the representation of historical trauma incites the reader to read the individual story as the representation not just of large numbers of people, but as a reflection on the entire human condition. Reading about the bombing of Hiroshima forces the reader to look beyond the lives being depicted, beyond the Japanese people of this time, and to think about war, nuclear weapons, and human responsibility and morality. The act of representing historical trauma, in and of itself, causes the reader to conflate the personal and the collective. Nakazawa adds to this effect through his unflinching depiction of the horrors of Hiroshima. His pictures show people with melting skin, with intestines hanging outside of their bodies, who become incontinent, and a constant flow of people dying. This may be particularly striking to the British or American reader, given the perception in these cultures of what is generally considered to be appropriate for children. The graphic depictions of violence and disfigurement might not, I would argue, be considered generally acceptable within these cultures. In this Japanese book created for children, there is little attempt to soften these images, or to protect the viewer from their horror. Readers immersed in this experience of historical trauma are asked to identify with the characters going through it, and then to extend that to imagining themselves, their families, and the possible mass scale of such an event if it happened again. This asks that the reader do more than read the book and reflect upon it within its historical context. Rather, the intent is to incite the reader to project the story onto his or her own life, and into a potential collective future.

The way in which *Barefoot Gen* asks the reader to identify with the individual story, extend that identification to the mass experience, and then extend that to reflecting on the reader's own life, creates an ideological position. It is a response to what Nakazawa noticed, that young people and teachers were not aware of what happened in the war, and asks them to read this story of Gen and see it as the story of the Japanese people in Hiroshima during this time. As a translation for the US and UK markets, it challenges the historical assertion that dropping the atomic bomb was done for the greater good, and was a necessary act to end the war. If these readers identify with Gen and what he and his family experienced, it makes it much more difficult to accept this ideological position.

The *Gen* books have been published with an overtly didactic message. And while *Gen* offers a fictionalised account, in the end it purports to truthfully represent what life was like after the bombing of Hiroshima. As Barbara Reynolds writes in the foreword to the second and third volumes:

> If you read Volume I of *Barefoot Gen*, you already know that this is not an ordinary comic book. In the first place, it is true. Everything that Keiji Nakazawa describes really happened - to him or to people like you and like me. And it happened to thousands and thousands of them, all of whom were plunged in a single instant from a known and predictable world into a flaming hell. (Reynolds,1990: v & 1999: iii)

The reader is being told that, though this book is fictionalised, it is true, and is asked to make the connection between the story of the individual and the stories of the masses of people who experienced this same historical event. The use of the narrative voice, and of Gen as an inspiring role model, all conspire to engage the reader to empathise with the story told, to believe its truth, and to hopefully act in the future in a particular way. Thus these graphic novels, based on the memories of the author but representing a large-scale event of historical trauma, use a juxtaposition of text and image in their attempt to elicit a profound response in the reader, going far beyond the focus back in time to the historical event they depict.

Bibliography

Bosmajian, Hamida (1983) Nightmares of History: The Outer Limits of Children's Literature. *Children's Literature Association Quarterly.* Vol. 8, no. 4. (pp20-22)

Lathey, Gillian (1999) T*he Impossible Legacy: Identity and Purpose in Autobiographical Children's Literature Set in the Third Reich and the Second World War.* Bern: Peter Lang

McCloud, Scott (1994) *Understanding Comics.* New York: HarperCollins (first published 1993 by Kitchen Sink Press)

Nakazawa, Keiji (1989) *Barefoot Gen: A Cartoon Story of Hiroshima.* New York and London: Penguin

Nakazawa, Keiji (1990) *Barefoot Gen: The Day After.* New York and London: Penguin

Nakazawa, Keiji (1999) *Barefoot Gen: Life After the Bomb.* San Francisco: Last Gasp

Nakazawa, Keiji (2005) *Barefoot Gen: Out of the Ashes.* San Francisco: Last Gasp

Pullman, Philip (1989) Invisible Pictures. *Signal.* Vol. 60. (pp160-186)

Reynolds, Barbara (1990 and 1999) 'Foreword', in *Barefoot Gen: The Day After.* New York and London: Penguin; in *Barefoot Gen: Life After the Bomb*, San Francisco: Last Gasp

Schodt, Frederik L. (1983) *Manga! Manga! The World of Japanese Manga.* Tokyo, New York and London: Kodansha International

Stephens, John (1992) *Language and Ideology in Children's Fiction.* London: Longmans

One Hundred Years of Children's Literature in Iran[1]

Farzad Boobani

In Iran during the past one hundred years, children have gradually come to be recognised as a class with an identity and a literature of its own. Two important revolutions and the political systems before and after these revolutions have played major parts in shaping this literature, which is now going through the final stages of institutionalisation, despite the still inefficient education system.

The history of children's literature in Iran in the previous century is closely connected with the various social, political and cultural movements in the country. Two important revolutions and the political systems before and after these revolutions played major parts in shaping factors that affected children's literature. It was, in fact, during the past one hundred years, that children gradually came to be recognized as a class with an identity and a literature of its own.

The Constitutional revolution and its aftermath (1906 - 1921)

In the early years of the twentieth century, Iranian society tasted an unprecedented experience. For the first time in its long history, the country was shaken out of its chronic political and cultural lethargy and started to move towards the institutionalization of democracy and liberalism. This historical transformation was largely due to the efforts of some progressive merchants, broadminded clergymen and, above all, a number of intellectuals who had been profoundly influenced by their contact with Western culture and Western thought (Ādamiyat[2], 1984: 3). As students and residents in the major European countries, these intellectuals had witnessed the deep changes that movements like the Enlightenment and the French Revolution had brought about in the West. On returning to their country, they combined forces with the other liberal-minded groups in the country and, in the course of time, Iranian society was pushed towards demands for its own rights and for the erection of modern institutions to restrict the unlimited power of the monarch and the courtiers and to reduce foreign encroachments upon the country. Among the initial demands of these reformists was the setting up of a House of Justice (*Adālat Khāneh*) to eradicate lawlessness and illegality. Later, the calls for reform were concentrated on one issue that could safeguard the fulfilment of all other demands: the establishment of a National Consultative Assembly (*Majles-e Showrā-ye Melli*) and the promulgation of a Constitution (Azimi, 1989: 3). This democratic national demand was pressed on the Qajar king from different sides and, finally, the Constitutionalists succeeded in making the king issue a decree for the establishment of the Assembly on 5th August 1906. In this way, the Constitutional Revolution, which had gathered impetus from approximately half a century earlier, achieved its main target and the country entered a new phase.

This revolution was, among other things, a direct outcome of the ever-increasing clash between tradition and modernity in Iran. On the one hand, there was the deteriorating Qajar system which, relying on foreign support, endeavoured to maintain its traditional framework of power and, on the other, the new intelligentsia that struggled for innovation and for the modernization of the country, and did not hesitate to question all dimensions of this precarious framework. The political, economic and cultural structures were thoroughly examined, and reforms zealously demanded. The advent of and advancements in the printing industry, emergence of the press, birth of movements in translation, development of urbanity and reformulation of the traditional system of education were all factors that accelerated progress towards modernity. This *Zeitgeist*, full of passion and enthusiasm for reform, affected the life of the Iranian child to a considerable extent.

The majority of children, and their families, lived miles below the poverty line. They lived in ramshackle houses under very bad health conditions; many suffered from malnutrition and were easily afflicted by infectious diseases. The educational system was ridiculously inefficient and learning, for the children, was equal to being physically and mentally tortured. Childhood had almost never been studied as a subject *per se* and children were, at best, reduced to 'little' adults with a great power to learn (Ayman, 1973: 19). Education was limited to the obsolete *Maktab-Khāneh* (schoolhouse), a dimly lit and unhealthy room presided over by a coarse instructor who had no formal degree and was often totally ignorant of the needs of children. For this instructor, the children were merely there to be taught the codes of *correct* behaviour. The material taught in *Maktab-Khāneh* was quite outmoded and incompatible with the mental abilities of the children. No scientific method existed for teaching the alphabet and the school curriculum was composed of difficult works of classical Persian literature and catechistic tracts (Mohammadi & Ghaeni, 2004: Vol. III, 38-39).

Before and after the Constitutional Revolution, however, the intellectuals - for whom progress towards a better future was a main objective - strived to improve the life of children. Some books on child health were translated into Persian and substantial steps were taken to modernize the educational system. Armed with the ideas of philosophers like Jean-Jacques Rousseau, intellectuals disseminated new theories of education, criticized the *Maktab-Khāneh* system and highlighted the importance of childhood for a society that had often looked down on the child as a nonentity. Ākhundzādeh and Malkum Khān, two influential advocates of modernity, published pamphlets on the necessity of reforms in teaching the alphabet and the establishment of a law of national education. Another intellectual, Mirzā Hassan Roshdiyeh (1850 - 1943), furthered their efforts and himself founded the first modern elementary school in 1888.

Despite all of its drawbacks, *Maktab-Khāneh* was the first place where children acquired some familiarity with literature. Along with the classics, the instructor would, sometimes, have the children study tales from folklore or religious legends and allegorical fables popular at the time. Such pieces later gained wide publication and became the first books to be read by children. The intelligentsia, nevertheless, turned the edge of its criticism towards these works as well because such books were believed to be vulgar and devoid of moral standards. For this group, one of the primary functions of literature was to teach ethical codes, and it was this didactic mission that eventually led to the creation of the first works addressing a child reader, which can be mainly divided into two categories. The first comprises simplified and retold versions of the great classical works of Persian literature, intended to pass on the national heritage to children in clear language. Some notable books in this category are: *Negār-e Dānesh* (*A Portrait of Knowledge*, 1883), *Masnavi*[3] *Al-Atfāl* (*Masnavi for Children*, 1891) and *Akhlāq-e Asāsi* (*Basic Ethics*, 1911-1913). The titles simply reveal the didactic stance of these works.

In the second category lie the books that were adapted or translated from Western literature. In fact, this was itself part of the greater translation movement that had started in the Constitutional era. Having a considerable impact on the culture in Iran, this movement facilitated the availability of works of Western literature to the Iranian readership, and translation was, speedily, turned into a medium that could buttress the repertoire of Iranian authors. For those concerned with children, fables by Aesop and La Fontaine proved to be quite workable, and translations and adaptations of their works were undertaken at once. *Farā'ed Al-Nasāyeh* (*A Treasure of Unique Maxims*, 1889), *Nardebān-e Kherad* (*The Ladder of Wisdom*, 1899), *Sad Pand* (*One Hundred Pieces of Advice*, 1895) and *Akhlāq-e Mosavvar* (*Ethics Illustrated*, 1913-1916) are a few of the works in this category.

Beside such books, children were exposed to the novels that had been originally translated for adult readers. Defoe's *Robinson Crusoe* (1719), Dumas's *The Three Musketeers* (1844) and *Count of Monte Cristo* (1844), Swift's *Gulliver's Travels* (1726) and Hugo's *Les Miserables* (1862) were among the novels that turned out to be favoured by children and adults alike. Based on these works, some Iranian writers began to produce novels for children as well, though these works, like some of their Western counterparts, suffered from poor characterization and lacked a well-made plot. A good representative of such novels for children and young adults is *Ketāb-e Sherāfat, yā Hekāyat-e Rezā va Robābeh* (*The Book of Honor, or the Story of Rezā and Robābeh*, 1900) which was influenced by *Robinson Crusoe*.

The Constitutional era was fertile ground for children's poetry as well. Although classical Persian poetry was rooted in at least 1000 years of tradition, up to the time of the Constitutional Revolution it was not easy to find poems written solely for a child readership. With some folk songs and lullabies excepted, almost no official poet had ever deigned to compose poems for children. However, with the Constitutional Revolution came a generation of poets who breathed a new life into the moribund Persian poetry. In contrast to their backward-minded contemporaries, these emancipated revolutionary poets were preoccupied with the ordinary people, their language and the democratic Constitutional cause. It is in the efforts of such poets that the roots of children's poetry should be sought.

Iraj Mirzā (1874-1925), one of the most outstanding architects of children's poetry in Iran, and a fervent supporter of the modern system of education, was among the first to write poetry for children and to turn his poems into a medium for educating them (Mohammadi & Ghaeni, 2004: Vol. IV, 539-557). Although many of his poems contained strong elements of didacticism, Iraj's simple language and the child's point of view he adopted directed children's poetry into a new course. He wrote poems on patriotism, devotion to mothers, and respectfulness to teachers, and his poems were immediately integrated into the textbooks for children.

Another noteworthy poet is Hossein Dānesh who published *Jangalestān* (*The Jungle*), a verse adaptation of some fables by La Fontaine, in 1911. Despite some difficulties in language, this volume was highly valued by and warmly welcomed in the modernized educational institutes (Mohammadi & Ghaeni, 2004: Vol. IV, 557). Children's literature had by now come a long way, but there were still miles to go.

The Age of the Pahlavis (1921 - 1979)

After the Constitutional Revolution, the Qajar dynasty could no longer stand firmly on its feet. Ultimately it received its death blow when in 1921 Rezā Khān, a Cossack officer supported by the foreign powers, staged a military coup and forced the young Qajar king to appoint him as the minister of war. Little by little, Rezā Khān paved the way for the termination of the Qajars and, finally, in 1925 he succeeded to ascend the throne of Iran as Rezā Shāh Pahlavi. From the very start Rezā Shāh had proved to be a dictator who longed to be considered as a saviour for the chaotic Iranian society. Of course, his great interest in modernizing the country resulted in some positive changes in Iran. During his reign the army was organized, economy was rehabilitated, reformations occurred in the educational policies and hygienic measures were taken to fight infectious diseases. But his flawed conception of modernity had led him to mere preoccupation with the façade at the cost of ignoring the internal deep structures. Most of the intellectuals turned into the opponents of his despotic policies when he set up a police state and imposed censorship on newspapers and books. To compensate for this unpopularity with the intellectuals and to earn legitimacy for its power, Rezā Shāh's regime sought an outlet in overemphasizing the cause of nationalism and the revival of the grandiose past of the country. Soon, sympathetic ties were made between him and the Nazis who had gained power in Germany and had adopted as a diplomatic strategy the praise of a superior Aryan race. This change of policies dissatisfied the foreign anti-Hitler powers on whom Rezā Shāh had relied at the beginning and, as a result, he was sent into exile.

The authoritarian regime of Muhammad Rezā Shāh, who succeeded his father in 1941, was as much inclined towards despotism, but its double emphasis on turning Iran into a modern country initiated some cultural developments in comparison to the previous decades. For instance, the number of schools multiplied, universities were established in large cities, literacy increased, modern theories of education were imported into the country, and, due to technological achievements, cultural exchanges with the rest of the world enhanced greatly. All of these factors combined in expanding the territory of children's literature to such considerable extent that it eventually entered its modern phase. In order to be internalized, this modernism was, like its Western counterpart, built on three distinct pillars: 1) new scientific approaches to folk and popular literature, 2) promulgation of theoretical and critical writings on literature for children, and 3) wide publication of original creative works by Iranian authors for children (Mohammadi & Ghaeni, 2004: Vol. V, 166).

Folk literature had always appealed to children but, for lack of a powerful theoretical background, it had never been used as a backdrop against which children's literature could be defined. Serious studies of folklore, however, started in the first decades of the twentieth century and, thereafter, children's literature strengthened its bonds with folk literature. One of the first intellectuals who played an important role in activating the potentialities of folk culture was Sādeq Hedāyat (1903-1953), to whom modern Persian literature is indebted in more ways than one. Hedāyat was the first intellectual to apply a scientific method for investigating into folk culture. He collected a number of folk stories and, later, compiled a collection of songs from the oral tradition under the title Owsāneh (Legend) in 1931. Some of the songs in Owsāneh are nursery rhymes for children and the rest include lullabies and song games.

Folk stories became an integral part of children's literature when Sobhi Mohtadi, under the direct influence of Hedāyat, started to narrate stories for children on the radio. He began his work a little while after the first radio station was set up in 1940 and continued for about 22 years. These programs were very popular among children and later Sobhi enhanced this popularity when he asked children from everywhere in the country to send him folk tales to be broadcast on the radio. By collecting and rewriting these stories, Sobhi made an invaluable treasury of folk tales for children. Some of his works are Afsānehā-ye Kohan (Ancient Legends, 1949), Dezh-e Hushrobā (The Enchanting Castle, 1951), and Amu Nowruz[4] (Uncle Nowruz, 1959).

In the academic field, too, some pioneers had started to disseminate new theories of child psychology. Among them, Muhammad Bāqer Hushyār, a university professor, translated some books from German and delivered lectures on children's literature. He also made contributions to Sepide-ye Fardā (The Dawn of Tomorrow), a magazine with a strong orientation toward educational psychology. Starting in 1953 with Āzar Rahnamā as its editor-in-chief, the magazine contained discursive articles on literature for children as a primary objective and it later issued a special edition on children's literature.

Probably the greatest contribution to Iranian children's literature was made by the authors who wrote the first original works for children. The first generation of these authors focused on the historical novel. Being politically disappointed when the Constitutional cause was lost under

Rezā Shāh's dictatorship and, paradoxically, influenced by his regime's exaggeration of the nationalist cause, they immersed themselves in fantasizing about the magnificent past of the country. Their works, combinations of fact and fiction, eulogized the splendours of the Ancient Persian Empire and praised the national heroes. Among these novelists, San'ati-zādeh Kermāni wrote novels like *Dām Gostarān* (*The Entrappers*, 1919-1924), *Māni-ye Naqqāsh*[5] (*Māni the Painter*, 1926) and *Salahshur* (*The Warrior*, 1933) for young adults.

The historical novel was supplanted by realistic novels and short stories when realism, as a movement patterned on European models, stabilized its position in Persian literature and, shortly after, realism became the dominant mode in children's fiction as well. Muhammad-Ali Jamālzādeh (1895 - 1997), one of the founders of modern Persian literature, is seen as a precursor in this field. In his story, *Sag Zardeh* (*The Yellow Dog*), published in 1942 and written for young people, he made use of an unprecedented narrative technique. As Mohammadi has observed,

> The setting [of the story] is a village...and poverty is [its] main theme. The relationship between mankind and an animal like a dog becomes the pretext for dramatizing poverty and hunger in the rural areas of Iran. (Mohammadi & Ghaeni, 2004: Vol. VI, 467)

But children's fiction had to wait until the 1960s to gain a unique and lofty position in its history. This uniqueness was, among other things, due to the efforts of Samad Behrangi (1939 - 1968), a great advocate of children. Like some of his literary antecedents, Behrangi was interested in collecting legends and folk tales for children, but his importance lies in his original and creative writings. Not only did this hardworking teacher rewrite folk tales for children, he also created stories of his own, stories which, for the first time, dealt with the experiences of the lower strata of Iranian society and drew a realistic picture of their poverty and painful lives. He chose many of his major characters from the masses and, in this way, made heard the ever-suppressed voice of the lower class. *Māhi Syāh-e Kuchulu* (*The Little Black Fish*, 1968), *Talkhoon*, *Afsānehā-ye Āzarbaijān* (*Legends from Azerbaijan*, 1965) and *Olduz Va Kalāqhā* (*Olduz and the Crows*, 1966) are some of his works. *Māhi Syāh-e Kuchuloo*, reprinted over ten times, gained the highest rate of circulation among books for children before the Islamic Revolution (Rahgozar, 1989: 52) and its illustrations by Farshid Mesqali won the Hans Christian Andersen Award for Illustration in 1974. (Abu-Nasr, 1996: 793) In his articles, Behrangi made severe attacks on works which taught children bourgeois morality and, insisting on revealing the inequalities and discriminations of an unjust society in stories for children, he strived to shatter the didactic mould of children's literature. Behrangi's writings were later associated with Marxist ideology and condemned, but no one can deny his great role in bestowing individuality and dignity on literature for children during the 1960s.

In the same period, children's literature in Iran made a great leap forward when two centres were established as its sponsors. *Showrā-ye Ketāb-e Kudak* (The Children's Book Council) which started its work in 1962 and *Kānoon-e Parvaresh-e Fekri-ye Kudakān va Nowjavānān* (The Institute for the Intellectual Development of Children And Young Adults), set up in 1965 were quite influential in organizing and promulgating children's literature. As Zohreh Ghaeni has noted,

> By holding sessions and seminars [on] children's literature... arranging children's book exhibitions...reviewing children's books and training librarians for schools...[these institutes] had a significant role in...the improvement of [the] quality as well as the quantity of children's books. (Ghaeni, 2006: 2)

The first seeds of modern children's poetry were sown by two groups of poets. In the first group were first-rate poets who also founded modern Persian poetry, and the second one comprised poets who wrote solely for children. Nimā Yushij (1895 - 1959), who brought about the most authentic revolution in Persian poetry, composed some lines for children as well. The first decade of Nimā's work in the 1920's has been described as a rather immature period in his career because he was still experimenting with the language and form of Persian poetry. But it was in the same period that some of his well-known poems for children were written. Two of these poems are *Āvāz-e Qafas* (*The Song of the Cage*) and *Bahār* (*The Spring*), written in 1926 and 1929 respectively (Mohammadi & Ghaeni, 2004: Vol. VI, 737). After Nimā some poets strived to open up new roads in Persian poetry. Among the first generation of such poets, Ahmad Shāmlu (1925 - 2000) proved to be quite innovative. Fortunately, Shamlu did not confine himself to writing poetry for adults only. In some of his volumes he created poems that were equally enjoyed by children. *Paryā* (*The Mermaids*) and *Qesse-ye Dokhtarā-ye Nan-e Dryā* (*The Story of the Daughters of Mother Sea*), written in the 1950s, were new experiments in blending the simplicity of nursery rhymes with the depth of a humanely committed world view. Shamlu even went so far as to inscribe *Paryā* with a dedication to a small girl: 'To the little Fāti Abtahi and the innocent dance of her dolls of poetry.'

The vanguard poet of the second group was Jabbār Bāqchebān (1885 - 1966), who also founded one of the first kindergartens in Iran. A pioneer in the fields of education, drama and fiction for children, Bāqchebān composed poems for the pre-elementary and elementary age groups. In his kindergarten, where he devoted his life to work with children, he combined education with games and entertainment, and encouraged children to recite poems or act in plays. In his descriptive poems, Bāqchebān put emphasis on children's immediate experiences in nature and with animals. Among his works, a well known volume of poetry is Zendegi-ye Kudakān (Life of the Children, 1929) and one of his most interesting plays for children is Pir va Torob (The Old Man and the Turnip, 1932).

Beside Bāqchebān, Abbās Yamini Sharif (1919 - 1989) and Parvin Dowlat-Ābādi also wrote for children. Of the two, Yamini Sharif was more prolific and drew upon a variety of subjects in his work, including nature, games, animals and objects from children's everyday experiences. The bulk of his poetry was, however, didactic and simplistic in its views. Of Yamini Sharif's 30 different works, the most acclaimed is Nim Qarn dar Bāq-e She'r-e Kudakān (Half a Century in the Garden of Children's Poetry, 1987) (Mohammadi & Ghaeni, 2004:Vol. VI, 787)

Children's poetry gained true maturity when Mahmud Kianush (born 1934) made contributions to works for children. He brought his valuable experiences as a poet for the adult readership into the world of children's poetry and enriched both its language and its themes. In his definition,

> Poems for children are like toys that are made of words, and these words give wings to their imagination. Children want to sing them, to dance with them, and to play with them. Therefore, the poems have to be musical, colourful and easy for children to use as toys. (Kianush, 2006: 1)

Kianush has published eight volumes of poetry for children, two of which are Tuti-ye Sabz-e Hindi (The Green Indian Parrot) and Bāq-e Setārehā (The Garden of the Stars.) Later, he published his seminal work, Children's Poetry in Iran (1973) in which he described the principles he had discovered and invented in his poetry for children. (Kianush, 2006: 1)

The final years of the 1970s were a time of turmoil and great unrest in Iran. Another revolution was on its way and the Iranian society was about to be exposed to some fundamental changes which would leave their stamp on children's literature as well.

The Islamic Revolution to the Present (1979 -)

The most vital aim for the religious revolutionaries of 1979 was the establishment of a governmental system based on the principles of Islam. Ultimately the Pahlavi monarchy was overthrown and, instead of it, the Islamic Republic of Iran was erected. The religious zeal which had been an essential factor in the Revolution, found its way into children's literature and, consequently, the first series of stories and poems produced for children were much influenced by Islamic values and revolutionary ideals. Thus:

> ...stories from the Quran, biographies of the Prophet, the 12 Shiite Imams...historical events, religious cities and shrines, duties and prayers, and teachings and deeds of holy men [became] the subjects of numerous books for children. (Rai, 1997: 31)

Rezā Shirāzi's *Quaribeh* (*The Stranger*, 1985), Rezā Rahgozar's *Teshne-ye Didār* (*Eager to Meet*, 1982), and Ebrāhim Hassanbeigui's *Amujān Abbās* (*Dear Uncle Abbās*, 1995) are just a few examples. (Rai, 1997: 31)

A short time after the Revolution, many hardships were imposed upon the country, the most catastrophic of which was the Iraq-Iran war which lasted for eight years (1980 - 1988). This event introduced a host of themes into works for children. The war itself, patriotism, bravery of the soldiers, resistance to the enemy and preserving the country's territorial integrity abound in the fictions and poems for children and young people in this period. Hossein Fattāhi's *Ātash dar Kharman* (*The Stalk on Fire*, 1988) and Nāser Yusefi's *Shahr-e bi Khātereh* (*The Unfamiliar Town*, 1994) are two typical works recounting the experiences of two young boys affected by the war. (Rai, 1997: 32)

The second decade after the Revolution was, however, a more peaceful time in which a younger generation of authors, accompanied by some of their older colleagues, 'focused more on formal and technical innovations and tried to subvert the dominance of the more content-bound works.' (Hejvāni, 2000: 27) Some of the outstanding writers in this decade are Mohammad Hādi Mohammadi, Mehrdād Qaffārzādeh and Zahrā Zavvāriān. Of the many volumes of poetry *Yek Sabad Boo-ye Bahār* (*A Basketful of the Scent of Spring*, 1991) by Afshin Alā, *Be Khāter-e Khorus-e* (*For the Sake of that Rooster*) by Shokuh Qāsem-nya and *Az Barg-e Gol Behtar* (*Better than the Rose*

Petals) by Nāser Keshāvarz are remarkable. Interestingly, some previously taboo themes, such as earthly love, were more outspokenly handled in works for young adults. An example is Khosrow Bābākhāni's *Mesl-e Dasthā-ye Mādaram* (*Like my Mother's Hands*) which is regarded as a step forward in introducing new themes into children's literature (Hejvāni, 2000: 31). Furthermore, the individuality and the autonomy of children and their participation in and criticism of the world of adults were generally more valued in the books belonging to this decade. (Hejvāni, 2000: 31)

Iranian children's literature has also gained international recognition as a result of works by some of its creative writers. An outstanding figure in this regard is Houshang Morādi Kermāni whose *Bachehā-ye Qālibāf-khāneh* (*The Children of the Carpet Weaving Mill*) 'was an IBBY honour book in 1982, and [he] was highly commended for his contribution to writing for children in the 1992 Hans Christian Andersen awards.' (Abu-Nasr, 1996: 793) Morādi Kermāni's *Qessehā-ye Majid* (*The Stories of Majid*, 1979-1987), a brilliant depiction of the experiences of a young boy who lives with his lovely grandmother, has also been translated into some languages.

Post-revolutionary children's literature is also widely published in magazines and journals. The weekly *Keyhān-e Bachehā* (*Children's Keyhān*), inaugurated in 1956, is probably the eldest, and has been followed by a good number of monthlies and periodicals. A watershed in the history of the press for children was the publication in 1994 of *Āftābgardān* (*The Sun Flower*), the first newspaper for children.

Such movements, accompanied by the increasing number of critical studies, exhibitions, film festivals, and cultural centres for children, point to the fact that children's literature in Iran appears to be going through the final stages of institutionalization. However, fundamental transformations in the still inefficient system of education, emergence of a true multiplicity of voices, dissemination of unbiased objective studies and activities and the establishment of children's literature as a field of study at the universities, seem to be some of the major prerequisites for children's literature to have truly come of age in Iran.

Notes

1. In writing this paper I have drawn heavily upon the following reference, some parts of which I have, directly or indirectly, translated into English: Mohammadi, Mohammad Hādi and Ghaeni, Zohreh (2004) *Tārikh-e Adabyāt-e Kudakān-e Iran* (*The History of*

Children's Literature in Iran). Tehran: Chista Publishers, Vols. III - VII.

2. The signs "Ā / ā" should be pronounced as the vowel /a/ in *father*. The sign "-e", wherever it occurs, should be pronounced as the vowel /e/ in *ten*.

3. Masnavi, (also Mathnavi,) literally meaning a couplet, is the title of a work by Rumi (1225 - 1293 A. D.), the great Iranian mystical poet. It is a collection of allegorical tales in verse.

4. Nowruz (new day) coinciding with the coming of the Spring, denotes the beginning of the new year in Iran. Amu Nowruz is a traditional figure supposed to be the harbinger of the new year.

5. Māni, or Manichaeus, (216? - 276? A. D.), was a Persian prophet whose religious philosophy combined Zoroastrian, Gnostic Christian, and pagan elements. He is said to have been an excellent painter as well.

Bibliography

Abu-Nasr, Julinda (1996) The Arab World. In Hunt, Peter (ed.) *International Companion Encyclopedia of Children's Literature*. London: Routledge, (pp790-794)

Ādamiyat, Fereydun (1984) *Fekr-e Democracy Ejtema'ee dar Nehzat-e Mashrutiyat-e Iran* (The Idea of Social Democracy in the Iranian Constitutional Movement) Tehran: Payām Publishers

Ayman, Leili, et. al. (1973) *Gozari dar Adabyāt-e Kudakān (A Survey of Children's Literature)* Tehran: Showrā-ye Ketāb-e Kudak

Azimi, Fakhreddin (1989) *Iran: The Crisis of Democracy*. London: I B Tauris & Co Ltd Publishers

Ghaeni, Zohreh. (2006) *Children's Literature in Iran: from Tradition to Modernism*
www.macondo.nu/intro_iran.htm
Accessed on 12.02.06

Hejvāni, Mehdi (2000) *Sayri dar Adabyāt-e Kudakān va Nowjavānān Pas az Enqelāb* (A Survey of the Literature for Children and Young Adults After the Revolution) *Pazhuhesh Nāmeh*.

Vol. 6, no. 21. (pp25-47)

Kianush, Mahmud (2006) Children's Poetry in Iran
www.art-arena.com/cpoetry.htm
Accessed on 20.08.06

Mohammadi, Mohammad Hādi and Ghaeni, Zohreh (2004) *Tārikh-e Adabyāt-e Kudakān-e Iran* (*The History of Children's Literature in Iran*). Tehran: Chista Publishers, Vols. III - VII

Rahgozar, Rezā (1989) *Negāhi be Adabyāt-e Kudakān Qabl va Ba'd az Enqelāb* (An Overview of Children's Literature Before and After the Revolution) Tehran: Howzeh-ye Honari, Vol. I

Rai, Mansooreh (1997) The Iranian Revolution and the Flowering of Children's Literature. *Bookbird*. Vol. 35, no. 3. (pp31-33)

Greek Picturebooks in a Process of Change: Towards the Construction of an Energetic Reader

Anastasia Economidou

There is good evidence of a tendency among contemporary Greek illustrators to experiment with the word/picture interaction in picturebooks, and to opt for interrelationships that are not straightforward and symmetrical. These interrelationships are deliberately used to create ironical effects, to question the authorial voice or to destabilise the meaning of the written word or even of the story itself. But is such a development positive?

Contemporary Greek picturebooks are becoming increasingly varied: not only in their subject matter, but also in their written text, their images, and, last but not least, in the interrelationships of words and pictures they support.

This essay will focus on the interrelationships of words and pictures, since they constitute the point on which this particular form hinges (Bader, 1976) and will attempt to answer three interrelated questions: do the forms that the word /picture interaction take in contemporary Greek picturebooks differ from those encountered in older books? And if they do differ, in what ways are such differences related to the role of the reader/viewer? And yet again, can such differences be taken as a positive development in the area of illustrated children's literature?

Out of the recent taxonomies concerning the word/image interaction in picturebooks, the taxonomy of Nikolajeva and Scott (Nikolajeva; Scott, 2002), is a good starting point for an attempt to start answering the above questions[1]. According to Nikolajeva and Scott, the two poles of the broad spectrum of word-image interaction that can be observed in picturebooks are 'symmetry' and 'contradiction', symmetry being a more or less equivalence of word and picture, and contradiction, a maximal dissonance. At various points across the continuum between these poles, Nikolajeva and Scott locate the categories of 'enhancement', 'counterpoint' and 'contradiction'.

Bearing in mind the above categories, an attempt will be made to show that more and more Greek illustrators today tend to avoid symmetrical relationships and opt for complementary, counterpointing and, less often, contradictory ones. This has been a recent development. For, although the picturebooks that have been produced over the last thirty years in Greece exhibit not only remarkable thematic renovation, but also high aesthetic quality and an increasingly freer and imaginative utilisation of all styles of painting (Asonitis, 2001), the area of the word/image interaction has proved problematic. Based on a pedagogic approach to picturebooks[2], the prevailing argument was that pictures were merely a prop for the understanding of print that the beginner reader was tackling for the first time and should, therefore, be in the service [sic] of words not interfering with, but rather facilitating the understanding of their meaning. Only recently, that is over the last fifteen years, have we had signs that the above argument is being opposed by contemporary illustrators of children's books. As will be shown by specific examples, although the new generation of illustrators, but of writers, too, move tentatively and relatively slowly, compared to other European and American practitioners, they nevertheless move steadily in the direction of experimentation with the possibilities of the form and, more specifically, in the direction of more independent pictures.

The first example of innovative illustration that is worth concentrating on is a picturebook called *Who Peed in the Mississippi?* (text by Eugene Trivizas, illustrations by Kelly Matathia Kovo) that was published in 2000.

There are three aspects of the particular book that give it its innovative character. First, it is the significantly enhancing and complementary interrelationship that is developed between the words and the pictures on most of its pages. Apart from complementing narrative information, the pictures complement the text in one more significant way: they establish the humorous tone of the story. Let us have a look at the first page of the book; read on its own the text is not funny: it tells, in rhyme, of a company of cheerful ducks that on a sunny day set off in a riverboat on a voyage along the Mississippi.

The role of the readers/viewers is central here. For the effect of the page becomes comic only if the readers observe the picture, notice the paradoxical appearance of the boat and appreciate the joke, that is, the fact, that the boat is called 'Quak' and that it is moving not only with the help of its wheel, but also with the help of the ducks' feet that are protruding from its bottom.

The second aspect worth noticing of the illustrating strategy used in many pages of the book is the excess of pictorial information. The first page that the readers encounter is a typical example: the picture, cluttered as it is with numerous characters, that is, ducks travelling on board the riverboat, accumulates information that is excessive compared to the text.

Thus, the text may describe what *some* of the ducks are doing on the deck but the picture depicts much more than that. The readers are in that way asked to pick out which of the pictorial information is relevant to the text and which is not, and to then observe all the little humorous details of the picture that divert from it; in that way their imagination is encouraged to follow little independent scenarios that are only hinted at by the picture. The irony that is created by the particular pictorial details - why, for instance, a duck needs snorkel and flippers in order to swim - is the outcome of the picture alone, which is thus shown to be fearlessly independent of the text in so far as it does not hesitate to take the readers' attention away from it by adding irrelevant information and cracking irrelevant jokes.

What, however, most clearly indicates the widening gap between pictures and words and at the same time energizes the role of the viewer/reader, is the fact that the pictures undertake the telling of a running story, a story, that is of their own, of which the text seems to be totally unaware. Thus, on the initial page that was discussed above, an observant reader will notice that among the numerous ducks that travel on board, there is a passenger belonging to an entirely different species: a mouse. From that moment on, the reader cannot but notice its increasingly conspicuous presence on every page. Indeed, the mouse seems to be an indispensable participant in all the dramatic events of the story until, on the last page, it becomes the protagonist of the final picture and, inevitably, the centre of the viewer's attention. Meanwhile the text has not devoted a single word to it, professing utter

ignorance of its existence. The point of such a 'conspiracy' between the writer and the illustrator is the deliberate creation of irony, which is the third aspect of the book worth pinpointing: by looking at the pictures, the viewers/readers get to know more than the words seem to know and in that way they are positioned at an ironical distance from them. Irony in picturebooks, as Nodelman has shown us, is an extremely useful strategy in the reading process (Nodelman, 1988). In the case under examination, the ironical distance between picture and words, on the one hand, brings to the forefront of the readers' attention the fact that neither the words nor the pictures can by themselves show the whole 'truth' of the story. On the other, it leads the readers to a more energetic position vis-à-vis the act of reading, as they participate in the construction of the meaning of what is shown on the page.

In *Weekends*, published in 1998, the writer and illustrator Alexis Kiritsopoulos, an avant-garde practitioner whose work was a breakthrough in the late 70's, chooses to offer the reader elliptic rather than excessive information. The interrelationship of words and pictures on most pages is not simply one of complementarity, but rather one of interdependence. The readers have no other way to construct meaning but 'to read the pictures through the words and the words through the pictures'(Lewis, 1996,271). There are cases in which the pictures seem to complement a textual ellipsis which is of a narrative nature. For instance, the text in one of the pages states: 'we couldn't leave the ball alone all night'.

By showing the man and his daughter, the protagonists of the story, sleeping under the tree in the branches of which their ball has got caught, the picture takes up the narration and helps the plot move forward.

On several pages of *Weekends*, however, pictures complement an ellipsis on the part of the text which is not of a narrative nature: a picture may depict how the characters mentioned in the text *feel about* what the words describe and thus add psychological and/or emotional weight to the text. Thus, on the first page of the book, the text states laconically: "at the weekend, dad picked up the kid in the car." The

picture on its part does depict the actual scene of the picking up, albeit in a strange manner: a car seems to be floating in the air above the roughly sketched outlines of high-rise buildings. A man is keeping the door of a car open, smiling to a little girl who, arms wide open in a gesture of joy, is rushing in mid-air towards him. The whole picture bespeaks emotional elevation. Indeed, if we 'read' the picture in verbal terms, which, as Nodelman reminds us, is what we always do when we try to understand what we see in a picture (Nodelman, 1988), it seems to illustrate the expression 'they are in heaven'. Its relationship to the text, then, is more than complementary: it is interpretative. However, readers can 'read' the interpretation of the situation that the picture is offering them only if they 'read' it in relation to the text, or rather 'through' the text.

A final aspect of *Weekends* that is worth commenting on is its interesting use of narrative voice. As in all picturebooks, the two narrative codes, words and pictures, imply at least two narrative voices: the one who tells the story in words and the one who tells the story in pictures. In the case under examination, Kiritsopoulos experiments with the clashing of narrative voices by establishing two different verbal ones, a third-person and a first-person one, while keeping a steady third-person pictorial narrative voice. The text starts in the third-person voice that is typical of fairy tales, but mid-way down the paragraph switches to first-person speech in speech marks:

> "Once upon a time, there was a dad and a mum who had a kid. They loved her very much. 'My dad is the most handsome and the strongest and my mum is more beautiful than Snow-white and than the Enchanted Princess.'"

And so the story goes on to mid-way through the book, switching from a third-person to a first-person narrative voice, both of which are clearly established as belonging to a very young child, until, eventually, the

first-person voice wins the day. Meanwhile, the pictures stick to a third-person narration throughout the book, since they consistently depict the little heroine as seen by somebody outside her consciousness. Let us have a look at two consecutive pages: on the first one, the text states: 'at the kiosk, dad bought her a beautiful ball' and on the next one, it continues in a first-person voice: ' "and *we* played until it got dark." ' [the emphasis is mine]. Meanwhile the pictures of both page-openings depict what the words relate in a fairly straightforward way, thus developing a symmetrical relationship to the words. Such a play with textual narrative voices reflects, in our view, the writer/illustrator's attempt to faithfully 'transcribe' the speech of a very young child who undertakes to relate her own story in a supposedly objective and distanced style, as if, that is, it were the story of some other child, but in the process succumbs to the emotional weight of her personal experience and betrays herself by switching to the first person. At the same time, however, by keeping a steady third-person narration in the illustrative approach, it creates an interesting tension between distance and involvement, subjectivity and objectivity, a tension, moreover, that is of narrative significance as it allows the words to change the implications of the pictures and vice versa.

Another Greek picturebook that experiments with narrative perspective is *Red Lena and the Parrot from Mars* (text by Lena Divani, illustrations by Melina Desfiniotou), published in 2002.

Because of the cartoon-like illustrative approach of Desfiniotou, the written text in this particular book comes in two forms: in chunks of text, in big bold but varied typefaces, which consistently appear on the left side of the page spreads, but also in hosts of verbal fragments that appear in speech bubbles on the right side of the page spreads, on the side, that is, of the pictures. Although, then, according to standard definitions, *Red Lena* is an illustrated book and not a picturebook, still it allocates to its cartoon-like pictures an essential role in the narration of its story and in the construction of its meanings.

The first observation that needs to be made about the interrelationship of the words and the pictures in the book under examination, is that nowhere in it is there a symmetrical relation between the two. Words and pictures alternate consistently in the narration of the story, each taking up the narration from where the other narrative medium left off, each pushing the plot forward by one step.

There are many cases, however, in which the narrative connection between the juxtaposed text and cartoon is not obvious: the readers are in those cases challenged to find what their interrelationship is.

What, however, gives *Red Lena and the Parrot from Mars* its innovative character is the play with narrative voices that the word/picture interaction brings to the foreground. An initial observation is that both the text and the pictures focus on Lena: the words talk about her while the pictures depict her in her everyday environment. In both cases, that is, there is a third-person narrative voice that asks the reader to see the heroine from a point outside her own consciousness. However, very often, there is a difference in the focalization of the text and of the 'talking pictures' that appear on the same page, a difference that enhances the effect of the latter. Here is an interesting instance: the text focuses on Lena's *brother*, describing him as a jealous nuisance who is keen on stealing his sister's things. The picture, on its part, focuses on Lena herself and in particular on her own sentiments vis-à-vis her brother; sitting at the table and slapping her brother's hand away from her French fries, Lena concludes: ' " Do you want to have a little brother? Don't ask your mother to have one for you. Take ours." ' Such double focalization as the one observed here inevitably leads to an

increased awareness on the part of the readers, who are invited to synthesize the conclusions they draw from the textual and the visual information.

An interesting aspect of the above remark by the heroine is that it is addressed to the readers. Indeed, some of the heroine's remarks in bubbles, but also the text itself, often address the readers directly in the second-person. 'Once upon a time, that is, *now*, there lived in a town, that is, *your* town, a little girl called Lena', is how the story starts, landing the fictional story in the here and now of its readers and at the same time de-constructing the story, in a typically meta-fictional way (Waugh, 1984). From that moment on, the flow of the third-person narrative gets interrupted again and again; the narrator turns to the readers and addresses them with remarks such as 'you understand why, don't you?' or 'do you see how easy it is?' In that way, the words create a confidential and often conspiratorial tone while speaking, in the voice of a peer, to the readers. At the same time, however, such exclamations and remarks bring the fictionality of the story to the forefront of the readers' attention.

A slightly different effect is created in two pages, where it is not the textual narrator who addresses the readers, but Lena herself looking straight at them from across the page. In the second page of the book, where the textual narrator presents the heroine to the readers, one reads: 'It was said that her hair was more red than tomatoes, than beetroot, than cherries, than watermelons, than strawberries, than apples.'

The corresponding picture depicts Lena herself posing, as it appears, for the beholders of the picture. This is the first full view that the readers have of her and it clearly aims at focusing on her red hair since her head is disproportionately big compared to her legs. Lena is facing the readers with an expression of wonder and addresses them thus: ' "Why are you staring like that? Haven't you seen red hair before?" ' Such an illustrative stratagem has multiple effects. To start with, the heroine's scolding remark reveals her awareness of the fact that she is being looked at, and, consequently, her awareness of her role as the heroine of a story that is being read. Her remark, then, as well as her glance at the hypothetical readers/viewers, bridges the ontological gap between fiction and reality: by addressing them, Lena steps out of her role as a fictional heroine and invites them, so to speak, to treat her as one of them.

It is worth noting that the above interrelationship of verbal and visual text is in effect an interrelationship, or rather a clash of narrative voices. To make that clearer, let us have a look at the one after the next page where the text concludes: 'Well, really, what the heck, wasn't there anything good about that girl?' while the picture next to it shows the smiling protagonist holding a huge heart-shaped balloon and saying:

' "Come on, are you serious? Everybody knows that I am a big-hearted person." ' The use of the personal pronoun 'I' in Lena's remark creates an interesting contrast, for while the text speaks *about* her, the picture gives the floor to the heroine to defend herself. This fluctuation between the 'she' and the 'I' of the heroine raises the question of the authority of the narrative voice of the story; it also raises certain relevant questions that are essential to every act of narration: for instance, isn't the narrator of a story supposed to know all about its characters? Can the characters step out of the narration of their own story and speak themselves? Can, in other words, the characters exist outside the imagination of their author?

Such implied questions that pertain to the nature of the narrative act in general, in combination with the alienation effect of the textual narrative voice, make *Red Lena and the Parrot from Mars* a children's book that seeks the same ends as many innovative, and in particular, meta-fictional literary texts for adults.

A similarly innovative approach to illustration, but also to children's literature in general, is encountered in the work of Vasilis Papatsarouhas. The way he illustrated Argiro Kokoreli's story *Playing with the Wolf* (2004) serves as an indicative example both of his approach and of the tendencies we are discussing.

The first line one reads when opening the book goes like this: 'Says her godfather to Anastasia: 'Shall we play the wolf and the piglet?' 'Yes, Yes!' cries Anastasia clapping her hands with joy.'

As is suggested by the opening lines and as is also implied by the title, this is the story of a very young girl and her godfather acting the roles of well-known fairy-tale heroes. What the readers realise, as they read on, is that the two players change roles all the time; now he is the wolf and she is the piglet, then they swap roles; then they both 'become' piglets and then again they both 'become' wolves. The illustrator does his best to create the atmosphere of joyful playfulness that characterizes the play of the two characters. Indeed, most of the pages depict movement and action: people, animals and objects are walking, tumbling, jumping, floating in the air. The very playfulness, however, of the illustrations is what makes their reading challenging for young readers.

που μπουσουλάνε, γρυλίζουν χαρούμενα, δίνουν φιλάκια,
μούτς μούτς το ένα στο άλλο, τρίβουν τις μυτούλες τους,
τρώνε από το ίδιο πιάτο.

First of all, in most of the pictures, Papatsarouhas chooses to depict not only the 'real' characters involved in the play, but also the imaginary wolf and piglet, the roles, that is, that the 'real' characters play. Moreover, he does not keep the 'real' and the imaginary characters separate, using, for instance, different illustrating techniques for each. Within the fictional world of the story, then, the illustrator bridges the ontological gap between reality and imagination, a gap, however, which is clearly demarcated in the verbal narration. Let us have a look at one such page: it is the point at which Anastasia and her godfather both act the piglets and walk around 'rubbing their noses', as the words inform us, 'and kissing each other and eating from the same plate'. As one can see in the picture, the girl is sitting on the floor, while beside her stands a piglet wearing her godfather's tie. In one and the same picture, then, one has a 'real' character and an imaginary one standing side by side. That is indeed a challenge for the young readers for, only if, in the light of the words, they recognize that the piglet *is* the godfather can they construct the meaning of the picture.

The other significant aspect of the illustrating approach used in the book is the interpretative role that most of the pictures undertake vis-à-vis the words. For instance, on one of the pages the text informs the readers that Anastasia has accepted her godfather's suggestion that he acts the 'bad wolf' and she the 'piglet.' It also tells of *how* he imitates the 'bad wolf': 'he makes a terrible grimace, shows his teeth, moves his hands as if they were ears and howls: 'now, I'll eat you up, little pig!!'"

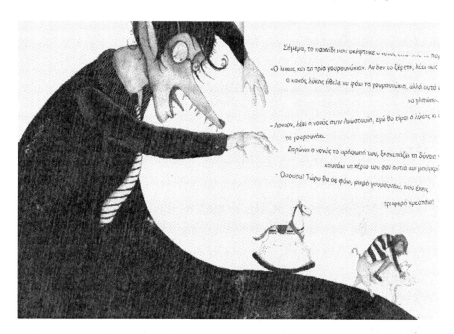

The picture, however, does not depict what is going on in the 'real world' of the human characters. That is, it does not depict a man grimacing and trying to look horrible, aggressive and threatening. Rather, by entering the world of the imaginary metamorphoses, it seems to undertake the depiction of the emotional impact that the particular role-playing has on Anastasia; thus, one can see a disproportionately big semi-wolfish and semi-human figure, wearing the godfather's spectacles and tie and stretching his arms in a threatening way towards Anastasia who, riding on a little pig and looking genuinely terrified, is on the run. Despite the illustrator's cues, the pre-requisites for the filling in of the semantic gaps[3] that are created in the relationship of the verbal and the visual text depict an experienced and critical implied reader. Only if the real readers are in a position to identify with the latter and fill the semantic gaps (Iser, 1978) can they realise that the picture reflects Anastasia's *impression* of the play and specifically the anxiety she feels while acting the role of the pursued piglet.

However, the interpretative role of most of the pictures creates yet another effect. For, whereas the words present the readers with what is going on in the external world of story, the pictures present them with what is going on in the internal world of the heroine. While, to put it differently, the third-person narrative voice of the text urges the readers to look at Anastasia 'objectively', the pictures urge them to look at her 'subjectively'. This, it must be pinpointed, is the reverse process of what usually happens when one is reading a picturebook. For, it is usually the words that create a subjective approach to the heroes depicted and the pictures that create the objective, distanced approach. However, the effect on the readers is the same. Caught as they are between a subjective and an objective approach to the heroine, they are urged to occupy a position which is the outcome of a critical synthesis of the two.

The need for the energetic involvement of the readers, and in particular, the need for their critical judgement is also prominent in one more work by Papatsarouhas, namely, his illustration of one simplified version of the Grimm's *Red Riding Hood* (2005).

As is the case in all classic fairy tales that are illustrated, the text here is realised and completed in yet another way by the different kind of pictures drawn by Papatsarouhas, thus making a different story. (Nodelman, 1988) What establishes the difference of this particular version is the intertextual strategy that is used in the depiction of the heroine.

Red Riding-hood is shown to wear the typical red cap that establishes her identity independently from the text. However, she is dressed in an unusual gown; it is a simple long-sleeved dress made out of printed pages cut off from what seems to be some older edition of the tale. One can actually read extracts from the tale on her dress. This unusual depiction of the heroine betrays the illustrator's intention to make her figure a visual symbol. In that way, however, he constructs an implied reader/viewer that *can* recognise the symbolic use of the heroine's figure and that *can,* moreover, recognise the particular interpretation that he himself seems to propose, that is, that the gown the girl is wearing is an indication of her past life as a heroine. Red Riding Hood seems to enter the present version of the tale dressed, so to speak, in her past, carrying literally on her body the previous knowledge the readers have of her. If the real readers are in a position to identify with the implied one; if, that is, they *are* in a position to recognise the symbolic weight of the heroine's dress, they will be reminded that this is yet another version of a well-known tale and that they cannot read it without inevitably noticing its similarities with and its differences from older versions. As Nodelman argues, in *all* illustrated classic fairy tales, pictures have an inherently ironic relationship with the text, simply because almost everybody who looks at them has both heard or read the story before and seen other pictures of its heroine. The readers' consciousness of the particular image of Red Riding Hood, then, as one among many others - and as a particular specific evocation of some vague words - causes them to notice not just the way in which the pictures show what the text tells them, but also the particularities of this particular interpretation of the text (Nodelman, 1988). In the case of this Greek version of the tale, then, by choosing to depict the heroine in the intertextual way that was described above, the illustrator is making a point of producing and stressing that consciousness on the part of the readers.

In concluding this examination of the changing Greek picturebook what should be pinpointed is that *there is* good evidence of a tendency among contemporary Greek illustrators to experiment with the word/picture interaction and, more specifically, to opt for interrelationships that are not straightforward and symmetrical but rather counter-pointing and in cases contradictory. As has been shown, such interrelationships are deliberately used to create ironical effects, to question the authorial voice or to destabilise the meaning of the written word or even of the story itself. If, then, there is a gradual development of a new type of picturebook in Greece, can it also be argued that such a development is positive? And if it is, for what reasons?

In his seminal work *Words about Pictures*, Nodelman argues that words and pictures come together best and most interestingly not when writers and illustrators attempt to have them mirror and duplicate each other, but when writers and illustrators use the different qualities of their different arts to communicate different information. (1988: 223) What, however, is one to understand by Nodelman's 'best and most interestingly'? For young readers, what adults regard as a 'good', 'interesting' interrelationship may be a very perplexing one; for the bigger the distance between words and pictures, the more difficult it becomes to construct the meaning of the illustrated page. To put the question even more plainly: is the difficulty young readers may have in constructing the meaning of an illustrated page good for them? It would seem, in agreement with theoreticians like Perry Nodelman (1988), David Lewis (1996) and Margaret Meek (1988), that it is. For, in that way, young readers are appointed the role of critical observers who have to compose meaning, not only by drawing information from both pictures and words, but mainly by interpreting the multiple and not always straightforward interrelationships that are each time developed between the two. It is good, then, in so far as it pushes young readers towards an energetic, meaning-seeking position. Of course, the idea that the reader is an active partner in the creation of meaning is not new. It was commonplace in discussions of both literature and literacy for much of the latter part of the last century. However, as Lewis observes, 'the composite nature of the picturebook brings the issue into sharp focus' (2001: 55).

Notes

1. For a critical survey of such taxonomies see Lewis, D (2001) *Reading Contemporary Picture-books*, London: Routledge Falmer, pp 38-45

2. David Lewis argues that there are three ways in which picture-books are often approached and analysed: the pedagogic, the aesthetic and the literary, the pedagogic constituting the picturebook as text for the beginner reader. (Lewis, 1996: 269)

3. Wolfgang Iser's concept of the semantic gaps created in verbal narration can be applied to the counterpointing and contradictory interrelationships between words and pictures. For, there, too, the readers/viewers have to fill the gaps created between the words and the pictures and thus contribute to the creation of the meaning of what is being narrated.

Picturebooks Cited

Who Peed in the Mississippi? (Greek title: *Pios Ekane Pipi sto Mississippi;*), by Eugene Trivizas, illustrated by Kelly Matathia Kovo, Ellinika Grammata, Athens, 2000

Weekends (Greek title: *Savvatokiriaka*) by Alexis Kiritsopoulos, Agra, Athens, 1998

Red Lena and the Parrot from Mars (Greek title: *E Kokkini Lena kai o Papagalos apo ton Ari*), by Lena Divani, illustrated by Melina Desfiniotou, Melani, Athens, 2002

Playing with the Wolf (Greek title: *Pehnidia me ton Liko*), by Argiro Kokoreli, illustrated by Vasilis Papatsarouhas, Ellinika Grammata, Athens, 2004

Red Riding Hood (Greek title: *E Kokkinoskoufitsa*), illustrated by Vasilis Papatsarouhas, Ellinika Grammata, Athens, 2003

Bibliography

Asonitis, P. (2001) *Illustrating Children's Books* (Greek title: I Ikonographisi sto Vivlio Paidikis Logotehnias), Athens: Kastaniotis

Bader, B. (1976) *American Picture Books from Noah's Ark to the Beast Within*, New York: Macmillan

Iser, W. (1978) *The Act of Reading: a Theory of Aesthetic Response*, Baltimore: Johns Hopkins University Press

Lewis, D. (1996) 'The Constructedness of Texts: Picture-books and the Metafictive' in Egoff, S., Stubbs, G., Ashley, R. and Sutton, W., eds., *Only Connect: Readings on Children's Literature*, Toronto, New York, Oxford: Oxford University Press

Lewis, D. (2001) *Reading Contemporary Picturebooks*, London: Routledge Falmer

Meek, M. (1988) *How Texts Teach What Readers Learn*, Stroud: Thimble Press

Nikolajeva, M. & Scott, C. (2002) *How Picturebooks Work*, New York: Garland

Nodelman, P. (1988) *Words about Pictures: the Narrative Art of Children's Picture Books*, Athens and London: The University of Georgia Press

Waugh, P. (1984) *Metafiction: the Theory and Practice of Self-conscious Fiction*, London: Methuen

Alex Rider: Mission Possible - empowering boy readers through fiction

Michele Gill

Anthony Horowitz's Alex Rider novels (2000-) have been conceived in a climate where 'crisis' has frequently been linked to discourses informing and recording the life experiences of boys. They are not traditional adventure fiction: whereas the heroes of nineteenth century narratives are assimilated into an Imperialist discourse which rewards them for their successful performance of Empire masculinity, there are no such certainties in Alex's post-modern landscape. Ultimately Horowitz leaves the reader without a final resolution. He introduces problematic discourses around masculinity configurations which are emphasised because of their juxtaposition in such a traditionally male genre, and yet the narratives potentially act as sites of empowerment for boy readers.

His last report had said it all:
Alex continues to spend more time out of school than in it, and if this carries on, he might as well forget his GCSEs. Although he cannot be blamed for what seems to be a catalogue of medical problems, if he falls any further behind, I fear he may disappear altogether. (Horowitz, 2004: 9)

The end came quickly on Air Force One...Cray was punching the side of Alex's head again and again. Alex still clung to the gun, but his grip was weakening. He finally fell back, bloody and exhausted. His face was bruised, his eyes half closed...Cray raised the gun one last time...And that   was when Alex rose up... (Horowitz, 2003: 312-3)

In Alex Rider, Anthony Horowitz has created the most contemporary of boy heroes who simultaneously resonates with images of a long established tradition of boys' adventure stories. Like many of his fictional antecedents, Alex is at once ordinary or at least distinctly average where school is concerned, but also absolutely extraordinary. The fictional adults who people his world, whether allies or enemies, manipulate him, abandon him, and try to kill him, but each time he comes back, he survives, he gets stronger...

The Alex Rider novels are currently a series of six adventure narratives from author Anthony Horowitz. Published annually from 2000, they have been conceived in a climate where 'crisis' has frequently been linked to discourses informing and recording the life experiences of boys, both in the popular press and in academic circles. In this paper I address Horowitz's construction of Alex in relation to 'crisis'. In particular, I examine the idea of empowerment for young male readers through fictional narrative, specifically, their relationship to the journey that Alex takes on his quest for survival. In doing so I highlight the constructions of masculinity that are represented in the texts and consider how Horowitz employs these configurations in order to re-enforce or challenge contemporary cultural understandings about the socialisation of boys. Although the novels have been heralded as exciting, adventure-driven narratives, they potentially offer up competing discourses surrounding boys and masculinities. Alex is both an ordinary schoolboy, struggling to keep up with his academic work, as well as a teenage spy who saves the world. In the context of 'crisis' and the foregrounding of problems in boys' education, the representation of empowerment which Alex offers to potential boy readers of the novels is significant.

Subverting power

The reader first encounters Alex as he learns that his uncle, with whom he has been living since the death of his parents, has been killed - ostensibly in a car accident. In the light of the bereavement and the uncertain future Alex faces, it is tempting to suggest that Horowitz's narratives represent an imaginary landscape of adventure for Alex; that Alex constructs this alternative world through his own imagination, drawing on knowledge from a collective and accumulated Western history of adventure. However, to explain away Alex's adventures as the product of his imagination reduces the potential of their impact for the reader engaged with Alex's struggles and triumphs. The potency of Horowitz's narratives lies in the possibility of Alex overcoming 'real' fictional foes within the contexts of the novels; he stands for the child who outwits the adults who threaten him and take some control over his destiny.

Bakhtin's theory of the carnivalesque, a space in which the established order is reversed and society's rules overturned, can be applied to Alex's fictional world in that he is constructed within a landscape where he is able to change the rules to some degree. Maria Nikolajeva suggests in relation to carnival theory:

> The child may be placed in a number of extraordinary situations, such as war or revolution, exotic, far-away settings, temporary isolation on a desert island, extreme danger (common in mystery novels), and so on. All these conditions empower the fictional child, and even though the protagonist is most frequently brought back to

the security of home and parental supervision, the narratives have subversive effect, showing that the rules imposed on the child by the adults are in fact arbitrary. (Nikolajeva, 2003: 129)

However Alex does not return to the security of his family but is left in the 'care' of the ambivalent Alan Blunt and Mrs. Jones of MI6 who are responsible for placing him in danger in the first place. By positioning Alex as both dependent on MI6 yet successful in overcoming the challenges he faces through the assignments they hand him, Horowitz makes visible the uneven power relations at work in child/adult relationships in which adults are given control due to an assumption that they will offer care and support. At the same time he gives hope to the reader through Alex's triumph; he suggests it is possible to take control, to overturn authority, if only for limited periods of time or in specific environments as suggested in carnival theory.

A further example of the subversive nature of power relations and their fluidity within the texts is the construction of Alex's 'heroic' character. As a teenage boy, although he is physically strong, Alex recognizes that he is no match in one-to-one combat with a number of the deadly assassins he encounters. Horowitz consistently represents him as using his resourcefulness and quick thinking to get him out of trouble. Dudley Jones has suggested that while fictional heroes in twentieth century literature usually take on the characteristics of epic superheroes found in myth, there are other understandings of the hero, one example being the trickster:

A different group of traditional heroes - the peasant heroes of folklore and fairytale - could embody a subversive potential. If the peasant boy embarked on a heroic quest and overcame the various obstacles that lay in his way, he could claim the hand of the princess, and in due course, become ruler of the kingdom. Although the revolutionary implications of this usurpation were undermined by the incorporation of the peasant boy figure within that order, the subversive potential of the story signified the utopian aspirations of the peasant culture from which the story sprang. (Jones, 2000: 10)

Applied to Alex Rider, I would suggest that he is constructed to represent a number of the characteristics of the epic hero in terms of his physical strength, courage and integrity. However, he also demonstrates elements of the trickster in that his outwitting of the adults in his world brings a subversive element to the narratives, turning social hegemonies upside down; to triumph over adults gives him a sense of personal empowerment, upsetting the status quo.

Roberta Seelinger Trites has suggested that a significant function of adolescent literature is to consider the deployment of social power and where the individual fits into this structure, be that the fictional protagonist or, through him or her, the adolescent reader. She suggests that the literature functions to ask the question "Do I dare disturb the universe?" explaining,

> ...protagonists must learn about the social forces that have made them what they are. They learn to negotiate the levels of power that exist in the myriad social institutions within which they must function including family; school; the church; government; social constructions of sexuality, gender, race, class...(Trites, 2000: 3)

In Horowitz's narratives, Alex has already learnt the lesson that to remain alive he needs more than brute force to overcome his enemies. He also realises that, when necessary, breaking the rules can also help him. One notable example of this is his involvement with a 'real' version of the Gameslayer computer game in *Eagle Strike* (2003). He has already played with the game on a computer screen, a simulated version. He is then forced by Damien Cray to re-enact the game, but this time on a life-size set where the trials are real and deadly. At first Alex follows the rules that he used to help the computerised action figure overcome the challenges on screen. However, he soon realises that although the game seemingly allows the player to make independent choices about the path to take, in fact it is structured as cause and effect and that by undertaking one trial many others are brought into play:

> Every computer game is a series of programmed events, with nothing random, nothing left to chance...No matter how much choice you might seem to have, you were always obeying a hidden set of rules...But Alex had not been programmed. He was a human being and could do what he wanted...To get out of the world that Cray had built for him, he had to do everything that *wasn't* expected...In other words he had to cheat. (Horowitz, 2003: 184-5))

Alex, then, learns a valuable lesson; he does have power in his environment, albeit limited, which he can use to 'disturb the universe' when necessary. He does not always have to do the expected and conform; choosing another path is equally valid.

Power play

In positioning Alex as the focalizer for the narratives, Horowitz allows the reader to learn of the relationship with MI6 from his perspective and therefore empathise with his predicament when he finds himself blackmailed into working for them by Alan Blunt and Mrs. Jones. The effect of this is to undermine both the authority and integrity of the adults, creating a further tension in the texts in relation to the 'enemies' Alex faces in that 'good' and 'bad' become blurred; the prize of power and control the ultimate goal. Horowitz crafts a number of occasions when Alex himself has to decide between good and evil, or at least how he understands them. When he is sent to the Point Blanc Academy he uncovers a plot, 'The Gemini Project', in which Dr. Hugo Grief is replacing the sons of influential men in the worlds of business and politics with cloned replicas of himself, made to look like the boys, in an attempt to take over the world. Alex eventually comes face-to-face with the cloned version of himself and they fight to the death. In presenting this dramatic scene to the reader, Horowitz symbolically represents Alex as making a choice between good and evil within himself; he defeats the part of himself that is like Grief, that wants to conquer the world with the use of force and deception:

> He was looking at a fourteen-year-old boy with fair hair cut very short, brown eyes and a slim, pale face. The boy was even dressed identically to him. It took Alex what felt like an eternity to accept what he was seeing. He was standing in a room looking at himself sitting in a chair. The boy *was* him. With just one difference. The boy was holding a gun. (Horowitz, 2001: 274)

Horowitz also constructs a number of situations in which Alex is in the company of 'attractive' enemies and has to make a decision about his relationship with them. The enigmatic hired assassin Yassen Gregorovich fascinates and repulses him in equal measure. Alex knows that Yassen is responsible for his uncle's death but at the same time he appears to care about Alex's welfare, in stark contrast to Alan Blunt. In setting up these oppositions Horowitz problematises assumptions about right and wrong and who makes the judgment and in doing so, brings into the narratives a sense of instability. The 'villains' who populate the series are represented as flawed in some way which signals their ultimate defeat in the texts. The common theme which runs through their list of various crimes is a pursuit of power, a desire to take control. However, MI6 and the CIA also want to be in control; the only difference appears to be how power will be used, but this is relative in relation to the positioning of the reader in Western discourse. The authority and certainty of Empire which informs nineteenth-century adventure narratives is not present in Horowitz's texts. Margery Hourihan suggests:

> ...in our postmodern era, when the old certainties have been undermined by the Darwinian and Freudian revolutions, by the end of empire, by the brute facts of the Holocaust and Hiroshima, and by our awareness of environmental degradation, or, in deconstructive terms, when discourse has become decentred, the meanings of a particular version of the story can become unstable. (Hourihan, 1997: 108)

The fact that anti-Western sentiments are raised works to disrupt the dominant ideology of the Western metanarrative. However, because they are voiced by subjects constructed as bordering on insanity, and their plots are foiled by Alex, a British boy, the discourses are none-the-less seriously undermined and discredited.

The series as a whole, with its imaginative landscapes, resonates with images from nineteenth-century adventure narratives and 'Cold War' espionage. Alex exists in a male-dominated space where he has to use physical strength and resourcefulness to survive. As in the earlier adventure novels, he is working for his country, to uphold Western ideology against those who want to destroy it, and echoes of a colonial past are brought to life in an array of villainous enemies who are inevitably vanquished. However, as Hourihan suggests, a post-modern cultural discourse creates uncertainty which Horowitz accommodates in his fictional texts in relation to power structures between both nations and men.

Masculine power

Horowitz represents Alex as moving towards young adulthood, making the work of R W Connell relevant to the situation which is portrayed in the narratives in relation to the power structures which exist between men. While Alan Blunt is constructed as an unsympathetic character, he is also represented as a powerful man because he is privileged in relation to what Connell terms 'the patriarchal dividend'; that is, he has a high level of institutional resources at his disposal which means he is able to influence and control others. Because the pursuit of power is central to these texts, Connell's analysis of relationships between men and the negotiation of status is especially pertinent. He suggests:

> 'Hegemonic masculinity' is not a fixed character type, always and everywhere the same. It is, rather, the masculinity that occupies the

hegemonic position in a given pattern of gender relations, a position always contestable. (Connell, 1995: 76)

Seen in this light then, the narratives represent a space in which masculinities 'play out' or contest power conflicts. By representing both Alex and Alan Blunt as being in possession of hegemonic masculinities, Horowitz highlights the unstable nature of privileged discourse and the investment necessary to maintain dominant status. The numerous fictional representations of masculinities which people the texts illustrate the ongoing negotiation constantly in motion.

Alex himself is presented as ambivalent about his role in MI6. As discussed earlier, he is initially coerced into the organisation but Horowitz constructs the relationship as problematic; Alex is attracted by the excitement and power his position gives him:

> Sometimes he wished that the whole business with MI6 had never happened. But at the same time - he had to admit it - part of him wanted it all to happen again. Sometimes he felt he no longer belonged in the safe, comfortable world of Brookland School. Too much had changed. And at the end of the day, anything was better than double homework. (Horowitz, 2001 : 23)

Throughout the texts, Horowitz draws attention to the complex relationship between Alex and emblems of power, whether represented by other people or objects from the world of espionage. Alex's relationship with guns is symbolic of his ambivalent feelings about his role as spy; he is at once intrigued by the power of the lethal weapon and finds it compelling, but at the same time is repulsed by what it means. Each time he begins a new assignment he is given a number of gadgets by Smithers, the 'gadget man' in M16, reminiscent of the 'James Bond' novels. For Alex they are always made from things which a fourteen year old boy might own; a key ring with a Michael Owen figurine which can be used as a stun grenade; a Discman that is also an electric saw; a gold stud earring which is an explosive device; chewing gum that can expand and be used to blow things apart, known as 'BUBBLE 07'.

All of the gadgets that Alex is given are to help him survive, to protect him. They are not intended to be used in situations where he is the aggressor. He asks Smithers several times why he isn't allowed to have a gun. The answer is always that he is too young, although as Alex ruefully points out, he isn't too young to die and M16 show little outward concern about using him in operations. Alex does finally take control of a gun when he has the opportunity to kill the hired assassin, Yassen Gregorovich:

> Alex felt the power of the weapon he was holding. He weighed it in his hand. The gun was a Grach MP-443, black, with a short muzzle and a ribbed stock. It was Russian, of course, new army issue. He allowed his finger to curl around the trigger and smiled grimly. Now he and Yassen were equals. (Horowitz, 2003: 47)

Of course this is merely an illusion; holding the gun and using it are entirely different and Alex is unable to shoot Yassen. Horowitz here draws attention to the difference between playing with violence - as boys are often encouraged to do as children through the toys they are given, the TV they watch, the computer games they play, and ironically, the books they read - and the potential consequences of real violence. In a case study carried out in a London secondary school, Stephen Frosh found that many young men do indeed maintain their hegemonic status in relation to real or threatened violence:

> ...the complex relationship between managing to be popular and successfully performing hegemonic masculinity is demonstrated by the fact that many boys wanted other boys to consider that they were really tough, but not senselessly violent. Their accounts tended to indicate that they had, at some point, 'proved' their toughness and no longer needed to do so. (Frosh, 2002: 83)

Horowitz positions Alex in a landscape where it is not unusual for masculine identities to be established and policed through the threat of violence. The fictional world in which he exists is extreme; physical strength and aggression are common expressions of power. Alex himself uses force to protect himself, but the ultimate act of murder is beyond him.

Containing power

At the same time the tone which pervades the novels is 'playful', suggesting that while Horowitz acknowledges the problematic nature of constructing masculinities through physical aggression, within the fictional landscapes he creates this violence is controlled; it is indeed fictional. Horowitz depicts Alex as responding to much of the aggression he faces with 'deadpan humour'. This at once diminishes the seriousness of the fictional violence and serves as a reminder of its very nature; that it exists within an imaginative space. Thomas Newkirk suggests that there are a number of strategies used in narratives which 'contain' violence:

> The violence is made "safe" in a number of ways: by removing it
> from human pain, by withholding some of the graphic
> consequences, by interspersing it with humor (the jokiness of James
> Bond movies reminds us not to take things seriously), and by using
> it in the service of a good cause like saving the planet. (Newkirk,
> 2000: 102-3)

Horowitz frequently deploys humour in order to nullify violence; for
instance, in the way he presents Alex's reaction to the news that his
enemy, Julia Rothman, is dead. Mrs. Jones explains to him the events
that led up to her death:

> Mrs. Jones took up the story. "The platform underneath the balloon
> fell on her as she was trying to escape," she explained. "She was
> crushed."
> "I would have been disappointed too," muttered Alex. (Horowitz,
> 2004: 337)

One concern that has been expressed in relation to boys and 'crisis' is
the centrality of violence in many boys' lives; the relationship between
aggression and media generated violence has been blamed in some
quarters for the increase in bad behaviour. In commenting on the
relationship between the two, Newkirk suggests that there is no simple
correlation, an analysis equally valid in relation to fictional narratives:

> The alarmist claims about the effects of media violence rest on
> research that reduces complex narratives with multiple messages to
> simple "stimuli" that work automatically, like a carcinogen, at an
> unconscious level. Not only is the media narrative reduced; the
> young viewers too are reduced to being unconscious reactors with
> no interpretive resources. (Newkirk, 2000: 102-3)

While Horowitz does use the landscape of the adventure genre,
understood as a space in which masculinities live out fantasies of
power often established through physical force, to explore the question
of violence in boys' socialisation into hegemonic masculinities, he also
signals to the reader the fictional nature of the violence in the texts
through the use of humour. As Newkirk suggests, readers are
potentially capable of distinguishing between simulated violence and
'the real world'. The reader, then, can engage with Alex's physical
triumphs and negotiate the fictional violence without any actual
consequences. Horowitz further diffuses the potential of 'serious
violence' in the texts through his construction of the enemies Alex

faces. They are described in exaggerated terms in relation to their physical appearances making their ugliness graphic, which makes them more laughable then frightening. A succession of outrageous names further emphasises the playfulness of the narratives. Alex's 'sort of' girlfriend is, after all, called Sabina Pleasure (*Skeleton Key*: 2002, *Eagle Strike*: 2003).

Empowerment

The narratives represent complex sites in relation to questions of power and empowerment. Horowitz presents Alex as attracted to the authority represented by a type of masculinity embodied in Alan Blunt or Yassen Gregorovich because of the confidence it brings him. However, he juxtaposes this with a discourse which raises questions about the outcomes of aggressive, physical masculinity as a means of control. Consequently the reader may feel empowered in relation to Alex's success, his ability to overturn the conventions and regulations of his physical landscape but at the same time uncertain about the impact of the violence used to secure power. Ultimately, however, Horowitz suggests that these narratives represent imaginary, playful spaces in which the reader can empathise with Alex's triumphs over his adult enemies and turn the world upside down, if only in a limited space and time which in the discourse of 'crisis' is a powerful emblem for boys.

In summary, then, I would suggest that these narratives represent examples of adventure fiction but are not representative of traditional understandings of the genre. While the heroes of nineteenth century narratives are assimilated into an Imperialist discourse which rewards them for their successful performance of Empire masculinity, there are no such certainties in Alex's post-modern landscape. The boy reader travels on a journey of self discovery with Alex, which potentially empowers him while also illuminating the complexities inherent in making life choices.

Ultimately, Horowitz leaves the reader without a final resolution. He introduces problematic discourses around masculinity configurations which are emphasised because of their juxtaposition in such a traditionally male genre. The result is a series of narratives, awash with humour and pastiche, but which at the same time resonate with tensions, indicative of a society with more questions than answers about identities both personal and national. However, as a source of empowerment for potential boy readers, Alex Rider does indeed fulfil his mission and his return is eagerly anticipated.

> A splash. Steam. Waves lashing at the windows. Sunlight turning the water into diamonds.
> And at last silence.
> He was rocking back and forth, a hundred miles off the eastern coast of Australia. The wrong side of the world - but that didn't matter.
> Alex Rider was back
> (Horowitz, 2005: 344)

Bibliography

Adams, M & Coltrane, S (2005) Boys and Men in Families: The Domestic Production of gender, Power, and Privilege. In Kimmel, M.S., Hearn, J. & Connell, R.W. (eds.) *Handbook of Studies on Men and Masculinities.* Thousand Oaks: Sage Publications Inc. (pp230-248)

Bettelheim, B. (1976) *The Uses of Enchantment: The Meaning and Importance of Fairy Tales.* New York: Alfred A. Knopf

Connell, R.W. (1995) *Masculinities.* California: University of California Press

Frosh, S. et al. (2002) *Young Masculinities.* Basingstoke: Palgrave

Horowitz, A. (2000) *Stormbreaker.* London: Walker Books Ltd.

Horowitz, A. (2001) *Point Blanc.* London: Walker Books Ltd.

Horowitz, A. (2002) *Skeleton Key.* London: Walker Books Ltd.

Horowitz, A. (2003) *Eagle Strike.* London: Walker Books Ltd.

Horowitz, A. (2004) *Scorpia.* London: Walker Books Ltd.

Horowitz, A. (2005) *Ark Angel.* London: Walker Books Ltd.

Hourihan, M. (1997) *Deconstructing the Hero. Literary Theory and Children's Literature.* London: Routledge

Jones, D & Watkins, T (eds.) (2000) *A Necessary Fantasy? The Heroic Figure in Children's Popular Culture.* New York: Garland Publishing Inc.

Newkirk, T (2000) *Misreading Masculinity: Boys, Literacy, and Popular Culture*. Portsmouth, NH: Heinemann

Nikolajeva, M. (1995) *Children's Literature Comes of Age: Towards a New Aesthetics*. New York: Garland.

Nikolajeva, M. (2003) Harry Potter- A Return to the Romantic Hero. In Heilman, E. E. (ed.) *Harry Potter's World: Multidisciplinary Critical Perspectives*. New York: RoutledgeFalmer

Richards, J. (ed.) (1989) *Imperialism and Juvenile Fiction*. Manchester: Manchester University Press.

Segal, L. (1990) *Slow Motion: Changing Masculinities, Changing Men*. London: Virago Press

Trites, Roberta Seelinger (2000) *Disturbing the Universe: Power and Repression in Adolescent Literature*. Iowa: University of Iowa Press

Apocalyptic Youth Fiction and Limit: The Politics of the Outside

Cassie Hague

*When we imagine and portray apocalyptic events, we are
confronting a limit - a limit on our ability to imagine the future - and a
limit on our ability to talk about politics. Foucault suggests that limit
can function both as a principle of exclusion and as a moment of
transgression and that from each of these functions, a different
politics flows. A theoretical exploration of the dual function of limit
can help us to understand what it may mean, politically, to tell our
children stories about the end of the world as we know it.*

What could it mean when we tell our children stories about the end of
the world as we know it? I argue that when we imagine and portray
apocalyptic events, we are confronting a limit - a limit on our ability to
imagine the future - and a limit on our ability to talk about politics.

This chapter discusses how we can understand the notion of limit, what
it may mean to confront a limit and what the implications of this
confrontation may be in terms of our understandings of 'politics' (a term
I use in the broadest possible sense). The chapter looks at *Children of
the Dust* (1984) by Louise Lawrence, a short novel written for the older
child reader which, along with a number of other books written in the
last 25 years, can be classed as belonging to a form of fiction which I
call 'apocalyptic youth fiction.' My suggestion is that apocalyptic youth
fiction's confrontation with limit is inherently political in two important co-
existing but conflicting respects arising from two different but related
ways of characterising limit. The first understanding of limit is an
'everyday' understanding of limit as a line, a boundary, a divide beyond
which we do not cross. A limit, in this characterisation, is what Foucault
calls a 'principle of exclusion.' Exploring the implications of this spatial
concept of limit can help us to understand the constitution of a
'standard' understanding of politics as the creation of political order out
of unmanageable chaos, as the creation of a social contract which
posits unified political subjects and limits the actions of those subjects
within certain bounds necessitated by the principle of state sovereignty.
However, there is also another way of reading limit from which a
different politics flows. Under this reading, a limit provides for the
possibility of transgression and for access to what Foucault calls
'thought from the outside'. Foucault's concept of 'limit experience'
suggests that it is possible for a person to go through an experience
which is so profoundly disturbing or stirring that it functions to shatter

the unity of the traditional political subject - the experience ruptures the sense of self as a unified being and clears the space for creating any number of new and potentially drastically different political understandings. I am interested in how apocalyptic children's novels can provide for *both* of these readings of limit and of politics. To explore this further here, I will first discuss the 'genre' of apocalyptic youth fiction, before moving on to briefly outline Foucault's discussion of limit as a principle of exclusion, his idea of 'thought from the outside', and his suggestion that 'limit experience' functions to shatter the political subject. In each case, I will make some preliminary remarks about how *Children of the Dust* evokes these two understandings of limit.

Ruins and dust: apocalyptic youth fiction as genre

"*Why* can't I watch television?" William asked.
"Because there's no electricity!" Veronica snapped. "How many more times do I have to tell you?"
"Then why don't you switch the lights on?" William said furiously. "Then we'll have electric, won't we? And I can watch television then!"
Sarah tried to explain. She told him about power stations and power lines and the effects of nuclear war. There were no mains services... no lights, no water, no television, no schools, no hospitals and no delivery vans. The world as they knew it was gone. William listened and questioned and finally, in his own five-year-old language, he understood. There would be no chocolate, no Atari space games, no trips to the supermarket, no cowboy films, no birthday parties and no Father Christmas ever again. Just ruins and dust." (Lawrence, 1984: 25)

Since 1945, increasing numbers of English language books have tried to explore what it might mean to live through a nuclear war. This tradition began with three books published for adults in the 1950s, *Alas Babylon* (1959) by Pat Frank, *On the Beach* (1957) by Nevil Shute and *A Canticle for Leibowitz* (1957) by Walter Miller. Importantly, however, there were, in the 70s and 80s, several books aimed at children and young adults which featured the potentially horrifying effects of the atom bomb (e.g. Lawrence, 1984; O'Brien, 1975; Swindells, 1984). The Cold War, then, gave rise to a vibrant tradition of 'nuclear' fiction, music and film for adults and for children, which was apocalyptic in tone and arose from the very real fear that the world was about to be obliterated by atomic warfare. However, whilst at first glance this apocalyptic 'thread' may appear to be solely a symptom of the Cold War, there has also been a wide range of apocalyptic novels written and published throughout the last 50 years and dealing with a range of types of disasters. Indeed, in more recent, post-Cold War times, the tradition of apocalyptic literature has continued but the cause of the apocalypse is now commonly climate change, biological warfare or terrorist attack (although some books such as *Cloud Atlas* (Mitchell, 2004) continue to feature the atom bomb). In terms of children's literature there have, for example, been books such as *Exodus* (Bertagna, 2002), *Floodland* (Sedgewick, 2000) and *Sharp North* (Cave, 2004) which deal with apocalyptic climate change as well as *How I Live Now* (Rossoff, 2004) featuring the after effects of a cataclysmic World War triggered by terrorism. There are also innumerable books set in a bleak and distant future, which feature a society shattered by undisclosed and undefined events (see, for children for example, Reeve's *Mortal Engines* (2001) and subsequent sequels). My own work focuses on this apocalyptic tradition as it appears in fiction for 11-16 year olds. This concentration on apocalyptic 'youth' fiction stems from my belief that the political ramifications of apocalyptic fiction 'mushroom' (as it were) when it is children and youth, the stewards of our future, to which we tell stories that feature the end of the world as we know it.

Children of the Dust is a short apocalyptic novel written for young teenagers. The novel, set at an unidentifiable time but written in 1984 begins with the fall of nuclear bombs on London and around the world. The novel spans 55 years and is divided into three parts each of which focuses on a successive generation of the same extended family living in a post-apocalyptic world. The first part, entitled 'Sarah' takes place in one room of a family house in the west country of England. It portrays the first days after a nuclear attack with horrifying and vivid intensity. Sarah and almost all of her immediate family suffer gruesome deaths from radiation sickness. The only two survivors are Catherine, Sarah's young sister and Bill, Sarah's father, who has by chance found his way to a safe underground bunker. The heroine of the second part, 'Ophelia,' is another of Bill's daughters. After a second marriage to a fellow survivor, Bill has fathered a child and Bill's new family live together underground, unable ever to leave the bunker for fear of radiation and the harshness of the sun. The third part of the novel sees Ophelia's son 'Simon' leave the bunker and meet Catherine and her mutant descendents out in the nuclear wilderness. This confrontation between Catherine's children of the dust and Ophelia's children of the bunker forms the dramatic hub of the novel. But the essential and fundamental dramatic *event* is the dropping of the atom bomb, the beginning of the apocalypse that results in the self-destruction of humanity.

Cassie Hague

Taking it to the limit: *Children of the Dust* and breaking down the exclusion of chaos from political order

> Sarah worried about violence and lawlessness, gangs of looters in a world gone mad ...The stench was indescribable ...blood and bones and the rotting remains of cattle (Lawrence, 1984: 46-55)

In many ways, apocalyptic youth fiction in general, and *Children of the Dust* in particular, can be understood as a reflection on the exclusion of order from chaos, on what happens when all of our social and political systems are destroyed. The first part of *Children of the Dust* depicts a Hobbesian 'return to nature'; as food and resources become scarce, life becomes a competition for survival with each self-interested individual ready and able to kill for self-preservation. When Sarah tries to find her sister a new home, she is confronted by Johnson who points a rifle to her head.' "I don't want to hurt you," 'Johnson says quietly, ' "but I'll kill you if I have to" ' (p65). Life in a state of nature proves to be 'nasty, brutish and short' for Sarah who commits suicide shortly after this incident. Indeed the very few people who manage to survive the nuclear winter outside the safety of underground government bunkers live in a harsh world of wild dogs and, a generation later, the children of the bunker emerge and attempt to reinstall order in the form of a military line of command. General MacAllister runs the military bunker and gives orders for the requisitioning of the outsiders' cattle. Faced with dissent in his ranks, he barks:

> "We're all British citizens and we need to pull together to get this country back on its feet. We've got no room for deviants! Those of you who don't like the way things are run will have their chance to voice their complaints when the new parliamentary system has been established. We intend to keep the spirit of democracy alive. That's what we've always fought for and that's what we'll go on fighting for! We, of the military, are here to protect the democratic principle." (Lawrence, 1984: 90)

General MacAllister's co-optation of democratic discourse is designed to provoke the reader, and this provocation serves to reinforce a perceived importance of traditional democratic political values. We are reminded of the necessity of a firm, rationally defensible, justification for the unified authority of a sovereign ruler even in a post-nuclear world. The novel, then, in its portrayal of the potentially catastrophic effects of the loss of political regulation and its affirmation of the 'democratic principle,' is part of a wider cultural commentary which tirelessly reflects on the origins of political order and sovereignty and which produces, organises and categorises commonly accepted political discourse.

The Theory of limit as a principle of exclusion: divisions and commentaries

In 1970 Michel Foucault produced his seminal, *The Order of Discourse*, stating that:

> In every society the production of discourse is at once controlled, selected, organised and redistributed by a certain number of procedures whose role is to ward off its powers and dangers, to gain mastery over its chance events, to evade its ponderous, formidable materiality. (Foucault, 1981: 52)

Foucault is consistently interested in how the production of discourse is socially controlled; how there are certain limits within which there are accepted and meaningful things that one can say or write. He goes on to take the reader through two major systems of exclusion - the prohibition of forbidden speech (particularly the prohibition of speech about sexuality, explored in later works such as the *History of Sexuality*, [1976]) and the division between reason and insanity [explored in his first major work *Madness and Civilization* (1961)]. Underlying both of these principles is the opposition between the true and false, or the tendency of society to forget how its claims to truth are a product of its own historical specificity. In response to the exclusionary principles he identifies, Foucault hopes to investigate how these rules and procedures function and how the discursive practices they create have come to be so fundamental yet have remained unacknowledged. In *Madness and Civilization*, for example, he asks us to listen to the silence of madness, to pay attention to the way in which it is silenced, and to try to understand why it is silenced. Influenced by Nietzsche's genealogical project to re-evaluate all values, Foucault, throughout his work, emphasises the ways in which society defines itself by means of powerful systems of exclusion - and then forgets it has done so. Society must ward off the criminal, the insane, the sexual - it must gain mastery over chaos and impose order by imposing limits on what we can and cannot say, be and do. *Children of the Dust*, then, in its depiction of a state of nature and attempted reassertion of political sovereign order, depicts the workings of a limit which can be theoretically understood as a 'principle of exclusion.' Under this reading, the novel is confronting a limit which evokes a simple either/or - we either have chaos or we have order and our response to chaos must be to reinstate order. In so doing, the novel is engaging with the limits that function to powerfully organise the major discourses of society and politics.

This political confrontation in part arises because limits are imposed on discourse from without. However, there is also an equally political sense in which discourse can produce its own limits internally. Foucault identifies three internal 'procedures for controlling and delimiting discourse': commentary, the author function and discipline. I want here to briefly outline one of these procedures, commentary. Foucault says in *The Order of Discourse* that:

> There is scarcely a society without its major narratives, which are recounted, repeated, and varied; formulae, texts, and ritualised sets of discourses which are recited in well-defined circumstances; things said once and preserved because it is suspected that behind them there is a secret or treasure (Foucault, 1981: 56)

He cites the repetition of formulas derived from religious texts as one example of the function of commentary, and the numerous uses to which the story of Homer's *Odyssey* has been put as another. Commentary, as just one of the procedures that limits and organises the distribution of discourse, creates tireless repetition and recitation whilst also representing the attempt to say something new on an 'essential' theme. Commentary aims to reveal a hidden deeper meaning to a well-known textual formula. As such, along with discipline, commentary is a principle or 'limit' that groups discourse; through commentary we tend to invest discourse with coherence and meaning, and to organise how it is possible for us to understand and classify a text. *Children of the Dust* and apocalyptic youth fiction in general represents a secular inheritance of biblical Jeremiad texts that warn of impending apocalypse as a result of God's wrath at the sins of humanity; a modern day commentary on Noah's Ark. But arguably they can also be situated as commentary on the 'social contract' tradition of Hobbes, Locke and Rousseau and can be thought of as thinking through the question of whether the principle of state sovereignty may be derived from imagining what it may mean to live in a state of nature.

Thought from the outside, limit experience and the shattered political subject

Apocalyptic youth fiction is inherently political, then, because it repeats certain formulas that allow it to reflect on the political division between chaos and order. However, these novels are also political in a different way and this difference arises from an alternative conception of limit and of what it may mean to be limitless. In 1966, Foucault wrote *Maurice Blanchot: Thought from the Outside*. He begins this piece by claiming that the statement 'I lie' is a paradox because it cannot be true at the moment it is spoken. The statement 'I speak', however, is demonstrably true at the moment it is spoken. Despite this apparent clarity, 'I speak' refers to, and is spoken in, a supporting language that pre-exists the sovereignty of the speaking subject, that pre-exists the 'I'. But, this supporting language is absent or missing at the time that the statement 'I speak' is spoken: 'I speak' doesn't mean anything other than itself. The two sides of the statement correspond so exactly to one another that they form a kind of vortex or void into which the supporting language disappears and in which the two sides of the statement endlessly refer to one another. Language is no longer the deliberate communication of meaning by a sovereign subject, it is no longer representation. Instead it is an endless, limitless 'spreading forth,' a 'formless rumbling,' an 'unfolding of pure exteriority' - it is language in its rawest state. Foucault says that it is modern fiction that language most often escapes the 'tyranny of representation;' it is in literature (particularly modern literature) that one can glimpse 'thought from the outside.'

The outside then, for Foucault, has a peculiar character which is very different to what we may mean when we talk about transgressing limits as 'principles of exclusion.' For Foucault, the experience of the 'outside' is not an experience that takes us outside in a spatial sense. As Widder (2002) claims, Foucault's outside is not an outside like one's garden is outside of one's house. Instead, it is an immanent experience, a dispersion of what and who one is, a dispersion of one's ability to act as a unified sovereign subject who can master language and meaning. The contemplation of the statement 'I speak' gives us an idea of the raw state of language and shows us the possibility of thought from the outside. However, in *A Preface to Transgression* (1977), Foucault also refers to what he calls a 'limit experience,' which he claims is another moment when we are shown the possibility of thought from the outside. When we undergo a 'limit experience,' we go through an experience so intense that we find ourselves in a state of 'ruptured subjectivity.' The term 'limit experience' was originally coined by French novelist and theorist, Georges Bataille. As Fred Botting and Scott Wilson explain the concept:

> The limits of thought and morality are shattered by experiences that exceed the bounds of rationality and utility. Extreme, intoxicating states of experience like anguish, joy, laughter, or horror draw subjectivity beyond the prescriptions of social and philosophical systems in a moment of contestation. These experiences release an energy that cannot be contained, cannot be returned to orders

based on rational or utilitarian economic principles. (Botting & Wilson, 2001: 18)

The extremity of the limit experience allows one to exceed the bounds of rationality and reason and creates a moment of contestation or tension that questions the traditional notion of, and all of the political preconceptions that come along with, such a unified and sovereign subject.

Thought from the outside, then, 'stands outside subjectivity, setting its limits as though from without...' (p15). Thought from the outside involves standing outside the unity of a traditional understanding of the human subject, experiencing how we are internally divided and fractured as human subjects and how different parts of ourselves produce different understandings of the world around us. Thought from the outside can give us a radically different understanding of what it may mean to be human than the understanding we get from positing a rigid, unified human subject. Indeed, thought from the outside 'stands at the threshold of all positivity, not in order to grasp its foundation of justification but in order to regain the space of its unfolding, the void serving as its site' (Foucault, 1990: 16). Thought from the outside functions to reveal how our understandings are historically constituted, how they are an attempt to impose order on an impending void or abyss but how this attempt can never be fully successful. We saw above how an understanding of limit as a principle of exclusion leads to a logic of either/or - we either accept chaos or we reinstate order. Thought from the outside, in contrast, leads to a logic of neither/nor. It shows that the attempt to impose order will always leave an excess or enigma, an 'outside' that, while it exists in a system, cannot be categorised under that system.

Apocalyptic youth fiction and the politics of the outside

It is difficult to show definitively that apocalyptic youth fiction provides the possibility of a thought from the outside. Foucault repeatedly says that thought from the outside cannot have its place identified or fixed and that every time you try and grasp this thought, it recedes. He says,

> The outside cannot offer itself as a positive presence - as something inwardly illuminated by the certainty of its own existence - but only as an absence that pulls as far away from itself as possible. (Foucault, 1990: 28)

Even if we are to find an 'outside' in the novels, Foucault is quick to remind us that this experience of the outside constantly runs the risk of leading back 'into the dimension of interiority.' (p21) This following section can at best, then, be tentative. Foucault does give us some hints, however. He suggests that to show thought from the outside, one must show that a novel is negating its own discourse and depriving itself of the very ability to speak meaningfully. What we need to look more closely at then, is the way in which chaos is constituted in the novels. I suggested above that the novels' primary response to chaos was to reinstate principles of sovereignty. But is this the only response the novels display? I suggest that it is not and that there are moments when the novels literally hum with the meaninglessness of apocalypse (a meaninglessness which invokes a powerful and important emotional reaction and which is only meaningless in the sense that it is beyond the possibility of being represented coherently in words). I suggest also that whilst on the surface, the political systems that the novels instate in the place of a chaotic state of nature reinforce traditional Hobbesian political and democratic discourse, on closer inspection, these political systems may simultaneously 'play' with the idea of the human being as a unified political subject. This needs further investigation than there is space for here. What is easier to suggest, however, is that the characters of these novels do indeed undergo a shattering 'limit experience;' the horror experienced by the characters is almost so extreme that 'it can't be lived through'.

In the first part of *Children of the Dust* as we have seen, the reader is introduced to child protagonist, Sarah, then proceeds to experience, along with Sarah, the graphic and prolonged death of Buster the family dog from radiation sickness, and the progressively worsening illness of her stepmother Veronica who eventually goes off into the wilderness to die. As the situation at home becomes unmanageable, Sarah decides to save her sister Catherine who has managed to avoid the sickness and we leave her as she is preparing to kill herself and her fatally sick five year old brother William with sleeping pills. As Sarah confronts her own death, perhaps we experience through her the limits of our own subjectivity.

> Sarah looked up at the blue heavenly sky. In the end people turned to God. But the death that would come was nothing to do with Him. He, and the world, and the whole of creation were about to be destroyed. Away to the north she heard a rumble of thunder, or maybe a nuclear explosion. It did not matter which. Nothing mattered anymore. All art, all knowledge, all civilization, evolution and aeons of time were meaningless now." (Lawrence, 1984: 13)

This is the first moment when both character and reader recognize all that could be lost in the event of a nuclear war. It is an example of thought from the outside in that it shows a desperate and meaningless void, but in showing this void, it also presents a moment brimming with potent meaning.

Foucault's work can help us to recognise that limit can function both as a principle of exclusion and as a moment of transgression and that from each of these functions, a different politics flows. *Children of the Dust* features a confrontation with limit in both of these senses of the word. Ultimately, it is my belief that a theoretical exploration of the dual function of limit can help us to understand what it may mean, politically, to tell our children stories about the end of the world as we know it.

Bibliography

Atwood, Margaret (2003) *Oryx and Crake*. London: Virago

Bertagna, Julie (2000) *Exodus*. London: Young Picador

Botting, Fred and Wilson, Scott (2001) *Bataille*. New York: Palgrave.
Cave, Patrick (2004) *Sharp North*. London: Simon & Schuster

DuPrau, Jeanne (2004) *The City of Ember*. New York: Corgi

DuPrau, Jeanne (2004) *The People of Sparks*. New York: Corgi

Foucault, Michel (1961) *Histoire de la Folie*. [Madness and Civilization: A History of Insanity in the Age of Reason]. Translated from the French by Richard Howard, 1967. Cambridge: Tavistock Publications.

Foucault, Michel (1976) *La Volenté de Savoir*. [The Will to Knowledge: The History of Sexuality, Volume 1]. Translated from the French by Robert Hurley, 1978. London: Penguin Books.

Foucault, Michel (1977) A Preface to Transgression in D. F. Bouchard (ed.) *Language, Counter-memory, Practice*. New York: Cornell University Press.

Foucault, Michel (1977) What is an Author? in D. F. Bouchard (ed.) *Language, Counter-memory, Practice*. New York: Cornell University Press.

Foucault, Michel (1981) The Order of Discourse in R. Young (ed.) *Untying the Text: A Post-Structuralist Reader*. Boston and London: Routledge & Kegan Paul.

Foucault, Michel (1990) *Maurice Blanchot: The Thought from Outside in Foucault/Blanchot*. Translated from the French by Brian Massumi. New York: Zone Books.

Foucault, Michel (1997) Interview with Michel Foucault in J. D. Faubion (ed.) *Power: Essential Works of Foucault* 1954-1984. New York: New Press.

Frank, Pat (1959) *Alas Babylon* New York: Perennial Classics.

Lawrence, Louise (1984) *Children of the Dust*. London: Lions Tacks.

Miller, Walter M. Jr. (1959) *A Canticle for Leibowitz*. London: Orion Publishers

Mitchell, David (2004) *Cloud Atlas: A Novel*. New York: Random House

Nigro, Raffaele (2005) Experiences of the self between limit, transgression and the explosion of the dialectical system: Foucault as reader of Bataille and Blanchot, *Philosophy and Social Criticism*, 31 (5-6), pp649-664.

O'Brien, Robert C. (1975) *Z for Zachariah*. London: Penguin Books.

Reeve, Philip (2001) *Mortal Engines*. London: Scholastic

Reeve, Philip (2003) *Predator's Gold*. London: Scholastic

Rosoff, Meg (2004) *How I Live Now*. London: Penguin Books

Sedgwick, Marcus (2000) *Floodland*. London: Orion

Shute, Nevil (1957) *On the Beach*. New York: Random House

Swindells, Robert (1984) *Brother in the Land*. Oxford: Puffin Books

Widder, Nathan (2000) What's Lacking in the Lack: A Comment of the Virtual, *Angelaki* 5 (3), pp117-138.

Cassie Hague

Widder, Nathan (2002) *Genealogies of Difference*. Chicago: University of Illinois Press.

'Nurs'd in ocean's pearly caves': The Limitations of Evolutionary Theory and the Fallacy of Free Will in Charles Kingsley's *The Water Babies*

Zoe Jaques

Kingsley was an advocate of Darwin's evolutionary theory, but in The Water Babies he suggests that Britain's upper-classes neither require nor demonstrate evolutionary development; for white middle-class English boys, evolution serves simply to justify their social superiority.

Critics have long recognised that Kingsley's *The Water Babies* (1863) embraces Darwinian evolutionary theory.[1] The recent entry on Kingsley in the *Oxford Dictionary of National Biography* summarises this critical tradition. It notes that he 'welcomed the publication of Darwin's *Origin of Species* in 1859 because it seemed consistent with his own idiosyncratic theory of related moral and physical evolution' but also argues that *The Water Babies* simultaneously mocks 'post-Darwinian controversies about human descent and distinctiveness' (Vance, 2004). This paper will argue that instead of adopting or mocking evolutionary theory, Kingsley recasts it to justify his loaded social agenda.

For Kingsley, evolutionary processes were primarily relevant to 'savages', those people from other nations and the uncivilised lower orders of Britain, especially the Welsh, Irish and Scots. The category of the savage was used by Darwin himself in *The Descent of Man* (1871), both to link humans across cultures and also to divide them into 'higher' and 'lower' races: 'The western nations of Europe, [. . .] immeasurably surpass their former savage progenitors and stand at the summit of civilization [. . .]' (p167). Although *The Origin of Species* (1859) is not directly concerned with the evolution of man, it too speaks of the 'lowest savages' (see p93, for instance). Kingsley, however, subtly alters Darwinian theory in *The Water Babies*, by suggesting that Britain's upper-classes neither require nor demonstrate evolutionary development. In Kingsley's apparent parable of moral evolution, environment, heredity, supernatural aid, and free will combine to shape individual lives, and for the target audience, white middle-class English boys,[2] evolution serves simply to justify their social superiority.

A basic summary of the plot would seem to counter such a reading. *The Water Babies* is the tale of chimneysweep Tom who slides through a maze of chimneys into the chamber of Ellie, a young lady residing in 'the big house'. Shocked by his own blackened reflection in her looking-glass and then taken to be a thief, he flees from the house. When he can move no further, he drags his exhausted body to a schoolhouse, but driven by a desperate desire to be 'clean', he washes in a nearby stream and is transformed into a water baby. From here we follow Tom's aquatic journey through stream, river and ocean, as under the guidance and nurture of water-fairies he learns to live in harmony with the natural world. In order for Tom to evolve further, however, he must first travel to the Other-end-of-Nowhere, and help his cruel former master. Only then can Tom become a true Englishman, making both his moral and physical evolution complete.

On the surface, Tom's working-class status is not a deterrent to his rise in society. Yet identity in *The Water Babies* is heavily shaped by considerations of class, and throughout Kingsley stresses the importance of environment in constructing an individual's moral as well as social self. Kingsley's well documented interest in sanitary reform is part of a wider conception of environment here.[3] Kingsley explicitly details Tom's lack of education alongside his uncleanliness, explaining that he: 'could not read nor write, and did not care to do either; and he never washed himself, for there was no water up the court where he lived' (Kingsley, 1994: 5). Tom's environment offers no cleanliness for body or mind, and fails to teach him basic ideas of right and wrong. His identity formation is entirely shaped by the behaviour of his master:

> [Tom] thought of the fine times coming, when he would be a man, and a master sweep, and sit in the public-house with a quart of beer and a long pipe. . . And he would have apprentices, one, two, three, if he could. How he would bully them, and knock them about, just as his master did to him . . . Yes, there were good times coming; and, when his master let him have a pull at the leavings of his beer, Tom was the jolliest boy in the whole town. (p6)

Tom's immediate surroundings impede his moral development; the slave wants to be the enslaver, subsisting on drunkenness and violence. His identity is further limited by his heathen upbringing. In Ellie's room he is baffled by pictures of Christ because he knows nothing of religion:

> He had never been taught to say his prayers. He never had heard of God, or of Christ, except in words which you never have heard, and which it would have been well if he had never heard. (p5)

Living in an irreligious environment, beyond the purifying effects of cold water and in the shadow of drunkenness, Tom becomes the antithesis of an 'ideal' Victorian boy. For Kingsley it is only natural that Tom should be horrified at the ugly, blackened sight of himself, as after all 'people's souls make their bodies, just as a snail makes its shell' (pp138-139). Both his inner soul and outward appearance are products of his environment. He is unclean inside and out.

Despite the debilitating effects of Tom's early debased surroundings, Kingsley demonstrates that changes of environment *can* have a positive influence. When Tom is first transformed, the Queen of the water-fairies declares to the other water babies:

> He is but a savage now, and like the beasts which perish; and from the beasts which perish he must learn. So you must not play with him, or speak to him, or let him see you: but only keep him from being harmed. (p39)

While his body has changed, Tom has not yet experienced a positive environment, and therefore remains a savage beast - in this instance, his shell does not quite reflect his soul. This environmental shift, however, offers Tom an opportunity to learn how to behave through his interaction with the natural and supernatural world. For Kingsley, Tom has a great deal to learn, 'he might have had very pleasant company if he had only been a good boy' but 'he was too like some other little boys, very fond of hunting and tormenting creatures for mere sport' (p58). Kingsley finds this moral fault inexcusable:

> Some people say that boys cannot help it; that it is nature, and only a proof that we are all originally descended from beasts of prey. But whether it is nature or not, little boys *can* help it, and *must* help it. For if they have naughty, low, mischievous tricks in their nature, as monkeys have, that is no reason why they should give way to those tricks like monkeys, who know no better. (pp58-59, italics mine)

Kingsley's stream teaches Tom this fundamental moral lesson. His identity and subsequent happiness are affected by his immediate environment and via the influence of his natural and supernatural watery companions.

So evolution alone is not enough to bring about Tom's development; it must be coupled with the education of a new *moral* environment to instigate change. But evolution has further limitations in Kingsley's narrative, as he suggests that while it might apply to the poor or foreign, it is not required for the well-born English. Amanda Hodgson has argued that an initial-letter illustration to the first and second editions of *The Water Babies* explicitly depicts Tom 'as nigger minstrel, a caricatured black man' (Hodgson, 1999: 228). Considering Kingsley's stress that at this stage in his development Tom is morally unclean, he is asserting a direct racial connection between blackness and moral degeneration.[4] Throughout the narrative, Kingsley links physical and moral degeneration to other cultures. He aligns the Hindu with the ape, for example, and also attacks the Irish for being morally corrupt. His parable of the wild Irish of St Brendan's Isle sees them all 'changed into gorillas' because they choose a life of violence and drunkenness (p118). For Kingsley, only other nations are subject to evolutionary change, and they are positioned far lower on the evolutionary ladder than fine English gentlemen. Tom's blackened exterior and ape-like movements place him firmly within this racially degenerate group; he cannot become truly 'English' until he becomes 'white'.[5] The challenge of evolving Tom, allowing him to progress, is ultimately to make him white and to raise him to the lower middle classes.

Of course, Tom still retains a part of his English identity. He is a 'little dogged, hard, gnarly, foursquare brick of an English boy' (p178) and 'a brave, determined little English bull-dog' (p86). Yet while Tom remains English beneath his sooted face, his poverty still renders him in need of Kingsley's social evolution.[6] Kingsley's water babies are human children taken by the fairies because they come from poor backgrounds and have existed in foul, immoral surroundings:

> there were the water babies in thousands, more than Tom, or you either, could count. - All the little children whom the good fairies take to, because their cruel mothers and fathers will not; all who are untaught and brought up heathens, and all who come to grief by ill-usage or ignorance or neglect; all the little children who are overlaid, or given gin when they are young, or are let to drink out of hot kettles, or to fall into the fire; all the little children in alleys and courts, and tumble-down cottages, who die by fever, and cholera, and measles, and scarlatina, and nasty complaints which no one has any business to have, and which no one will have some day, when folks have common sense; and all the little children who have been killed by cruel masters, and wicked soldiers (p122)

While such poor land children may require transformation, Kingsley shows that the upper registers of society do not; the implication is that they are already at the top of the evolutionary scale and have reached a state of moral excellence. When Ellie becomes a water baby, she does not undergo any character transformation. Her role is simply to influence Tom's evolutionary development and to be returned to her land body at the close of the novel - she does not change in terms of morality, beliefs, religion or behaviour. Sir John Harthover, the 'very sound-headed, sound-hearted squire' (p17), is subjected to even less development. He stands as a shining example of the fully evolved 'fine old English Gentleman', complete with a 'face as red as a rose, and a hand as hard as a table, and a back as broad as a bullock's' (p42). He is morally and physically irreproachable - kind and generous as well as upper-class and white. It seems unlikely, however, that this pinnacle of evolutionary development has been subjected to an apprenticeship as a water baby in stream, river and sea. Kingsley excuses his squire from the requirement of winning his spurs; the rich ancestral history of his house and name secures his position.

It is of course axiomatic to note that Victorian society was shaped by class concerns, and that science, particularly evolutionary theory, was used to embed such distinctions in 'nature'. But Kingsley takes the science of difference a step further in *The Water Babies*. For the working classes, he offers a limited evolutionary possibility: wealthy Englishmen, being fully evolved, have no need for it. In *The Descent of Man*, Darwin discusses the debate over whether all men started out as civilised and degenerated, which appears to be Kingsley's position, or rose from a barbarous condition. Darwin differs from Kingsley by concluding 'that man has risen, though by slow and interrupted steps, from a lowly condition to the highest standard as yet attained by him in knowledge, morals and religion' (p172). Critics have been split as to whether Kingsley's *Water Babies* adopts Darwinian theory or mocks it, not least because of the irony that often inflects his narrative. But despite his ironic and satirical tone, Kingsley rather recasts and limits evolutionary theory to suit his personal social project: redeem good white little boys, but don't elevate them above their betters.

Nonetheless, any consideration of Kingsley's surprising assertion of nurture over nature, for little Englishmen at least, must also take into account how his conception of fairy tale affects such a construct. Kingsley's meta-narrative is constructed so as to remind the reader repeatedly that magical interference is a fiction:

> Don't you know that this is a fairy tale, and all fun and pretence; and that you are not to believe one word of it, even if it is true? (p51)

Tom's progression, beyond the binds of his parentage and upbringing, is specific to fairy tale - it requires a magical transformation into a water baby that can never really happen. The supernatural assistance of the Irishwomen, Mrs Bedonebyasyoudid, Mrs Doasyouwouldbedoneby and Mother Carey are essential to the story, for as Kingsley glibly explains: 'There must be fairies; for this is a fairy tale: and how can one have a fairy tale if there are no fairies?' (p40)[7]

These fairies, however, also have the further function of nursing Tom through his evolutionary development and teaching him how to behave. They are effectively allegorical figures for the Christian supernatural, and as Colin Manlove points out, Mrs Bedonebyasyoudid and Mrs Doasyouwouldbedoneby function as natural reward and natural punishment, informing Tom's journey towards spiritual advancement in both body and soul (Manlove, 1975: 46-47).[8] But even such divine influence is shown to have a limited potential to bring about real change.[9] Kingsley subtly points to the fact that while the moral of his tale may be true, the fairy influence certainly is not - 'you are not to believe one word of it'. While his tone seems ironic, a point that Alderson notes (Alderson, 1995: xxiv), Kingsley is strongly encouraging his target audience not to believe in the possibilities of fairy-tale transformation. The little middle-class English boys who will read *The Water Babies* have no hope of such supernatural intervention in their lives. Each must rely on his birth and education for any potential success, 'and learn his lesson for himself by sound and sharp experience' (p59).

For Tom even divine intervention does not fully allow him to escape his class binds. He never achieves his one true desire - to kiss Ellie. When Tom first meets Ellie in her water baby form he recognises her higher social status, and limits his actions accordingly:

> "Dear me!" cried Tom. "You are the very little white lady whom I saw in bed." And he jumped at her, and longed to hug and kiss her; but did not, remembering that she was a lady born (p141)

Later, before he embarks on his journey to the Other-End-of-Nowhere, Tom is again unable to achieve his desire:

> And in the twinkling of an eye there stood Ellie, smiling, and looking so happy that Tom longed to kiss her; but was still afraid it would not be respectful, because she was a lady born. (p146)

Of course, the implication at this point in the narrative is that once Tom has completed his evolutionary development he will be fit to marry Ellie. Kingsley is certainly aware of this expectation, inserting the obvious question into the closing paragraph: 'And of course Tom married Ellie?' (p212). Such a conclusion, however, is not appropriate for Kingsley's social project: 'My dear child, what a silly notion! Don't you know that no one ever marries in a fairy tale, under the rank of a prince or a princess?' (p212) Under the guise of the rules of fairy tale, but with an emphasis on rank, Kingsley insists upon inviolable social boundaries.

Yet surely if this were truly a fairy tale, Tom could become eligible for Ellie; can not a frog become a prince? Back in the river, from where Tom has seemingly both morally and spiritually evolved, Kingsley reveals his social prejudice in the allegorical miscegenation narrative of the trout and the salmon:

> "Why, I have actually known one of them [a trout] propose to a lady salmon, the impudent little creature."
> "I should hope," said the gentleman, "that there are very few ladies of our race who would degrade themselves by listening to such a creature for an instant. If I saw such a thing happen, I should consider it my duty to put them both to death upon the spot." So the old salmon said, like an old blue-blooded hidalgo of Spain; and what is more, he would have done it too. (pp79-80)

There can be no marriage between a trout and a salmon, just as there can be none between a chimneysweep and a lady born. Although Kingsley seems to distance himself from the salmon's views, Tom is denied a similar marital advancement despite enduring the trials of the task 'he did not like' (p212). Valentine Cunningham has argued that *The Water Babies* is:

> one more among the scores of versions to be found the world over of what in Britain is known as the Cinderella story: tales of the neglected child who makes good after a period of difficulty and problem-solving, a testing time that involves consignment to the place of ashes, dirt or soot. (Cunningham, 1985: 123)

If *The Water Babies* is a Cinderella story, then it is a very limited one.[10] Unlike his contemporary, Curdie, the brave miner child from George MacDonald's *The Princess and the Goblin* (1872), Tom is not even allowed the prize of a kiss from his princess. Tom is instead rewarded by becoming an applied scientist, an undoubted improvement over his chimneysweep origins, but a fairly realistic one. Kingsley is here aligned with the schoolmistress who says to the exhausted Tom, ' "If thou wert a bit cleaner I'd put thee in my own bed" ' (p36) but proceeds to lodge him, 'in an outhouse upon soft sweet hay and an old rug' (p37). Like the schoolmistress, Kingsley sees Tom as not quite clean enough for the comforts of the metaphorical best bed; he keeps him in the outhouse, albeit a slightly improved one. This happy-ever-after firmly prevents too much escape from class limitations. Kingsley's refusal to allow Tom and Ellie to marry not only denies the structure of fairy-tale narrative but also counters natural selection. Kingsley's class ideology suppresses the potential for such selection by denying Tom and Ellie's union, which is in turn effectively a denial of evolutionary possibility.

Although it is surprising enough that evolution and fairy-tale narrative are shown to lead to such limited change, it is even more surprising that free will is exposed as a fiction. On the surface, Kingsley appears to suggest that choice, and in particular choosing correctly, is extremely important to moral development. Mary Hanawalt, for instance, argues that:

> Kingsley's plots are not deterministic. He recognized the influence of environment upon character, as in *Alton Locke*, but he made this influence secondary to that of the human will. Each one of his characters is represented as free to behave as he wishes, a result of the author's faith in the natural goodness of man (Hanawalt, 1937: 597).

More recently, Elaine Ostry has similarly emphasised the role of choice in Tom's moral development (Ostry, 2003: 32-35). Tom, however, is in no way free to 'behave as he wishes' despite the many illusions of choice which rest upon the surface of Kingsley's narrative. Mrs Bedonebyasyoudid, for example, explains to Tom that there is a second path of evolution for those who choose it:

> "there are two sides to every question, and a downhill as well as an uphill road; and, if I can turn beasts into men, I can, by the same laws of circumstance, and selection, and competition, turn men into beasts." (p152)

She explains how the Doasyoulikes once existed in a utopian landscape, yet their laziness and complacency led them to revert gradually to a savage existence before their race finally became extinct. It would seem from this parable that Kingsley emphasises the importance of free-will, suggesting that Tom must *choose* to become morally developed. But underlying this is Kingsley's assertion that one cannot choose goodness and that little boys must remain on their allotted paths to develop into good and morally astute gentlemen.

Kingsley's argument against choice is furthered in the story of the last of the Gairfowl, a bird who stands and complains on the Allalonestone, commenting that her species disdained the notion of development through growing wings:

> What can they want with flying and raising themselves above their proper station in life? In the days of my ancestors no birds ever thought of having wings, and did very well without; and now they all laugh at me because I keep to the good old fashion. Why, the very marrocks and dovekies have got wings, the vulgar creatures, and

poor little ones enough they are; and my own cousins too, the razor-
bills, who are gentlefolk born, and ought to know better than to ape
their inferiors. (pp158-159)

The Gairfowl's refusal to evolve leads to the extinction of her species.[11]
Amanda Hodgson states that this evolutionary error of the Gairfowl is
not physical but moral, suggesting that:

Here the Victorian myth of self-improvement crosses with evolution
to produce the key point of the story: it is up to individuals to ensure
that they develop in the correct spiritual direction, or risk ending like
the Gairfowl. (p235)

Hodgson also argues that this use of evolution relates more to
Lamarckian than Darwinian theory, proposing that:

although the text makes reference in some places to a Darwinian
process of natural selection, the evolutionary model it more
commonly espouses is a much more Lamarckian one... Change in
the novel, at least for humankind, is not random. The child readers
are exhorted consciously to work towards a spiritual transformation.
(pp237-238)

Certainly the potential for Tom to evolve into not only a greater physical
form, but also to higher social status, would seem to appropriate
Lamarck's theories. Lamarck's ideas centre on self development
through a conscious will to succeed, as he believed that animals strove
to achieve evolutionary change. Lamarck suggested, for example, that
a giraffe may have descended from a shorter-necked animal, yet due to
the need to reach the vegetation on high trees would, by stretching its
neck upwards, have caused more nervous fluid to flow around its body
and lengthened its neck. He ventured that this acquired characteristic
may have been passed on to future giraffes and caused the elongated
neck of the species. Lamarck's concept that free will alone could cause
physical change carried with it the implication, as Hodgson notes, that
anyone with enough desire and conviction could promote himself to a
higher order. This self-driven advancement, however, is not an option in
The Water Babies. Will and work alone will not transcend rigid class
lines.

Quite contrary to the surface construct that making the correct choices
achieves moral and physical progression, free-will, as shown by the
Doasyoulikes and Gairfowl, achieves nothing but degeneration or
extinction. Hodgson argues that 'Tom and Ellie and the other humans
differ from animals in the story' because 'they may choose whether or

not to fit themselves for this ultimate change' (p237). This also proves, however, to be an illusion. Choice in *The Water Babies* is always negative and only ever leads to moral debasement, for human as well as animal characters. We learn that Mr Grimes once lived in a morally good environment, and yet he chooses to exercise his free will, leading to a brutal, drunken and petty criminal existence. All of Tom's actual choices also lead to degeneration and require punishment, because every choice he makes is shown to be morally wrong. When Tom chooses to steal, for example, he is punished by his body being changed into something 'horny and prickly... just like a sea egg' (p138). This idea of limited choice is in keeping with Kingsley's assertion that:

> Evil, as such, has no existence; but men can and do resist God's will, and break the law, which is appointed for them, and so punish themselves by getting into disharmony with their own constitution and that of the universe. (*Letters*, 1876: 28)

It would seem, however, that positive choice must exist in *The Water Babies*; only through *choosing* to travel to the Other-End-of-Nowhere can Tom finally become a gentleman. Yet all of Tom's 'positive' choices are in fact compelled through supernatural intervention: 'he would never have found his way, if the fairies had not guided him' (p81). Such guidance even prompts Tom's decisions to repent bad behaviour. When he decides to admit to stealing sweets, he does so because he is miserable, but it is a misery derived from environmental and supernatural influences. He admits his wrong doing not because he desires spiritual and moral advancement, but because he dislikes the fact that his prickly body means 'nobody would cuddle him, or play with him, or even like to look at him' (p139). His hand, as it were, is forced. Even the ultimate choice in the narrative, Tom's decision to do the thing he does not like and help Mr Grimes, is shown to be necessity, as Mrs Bedonebyasyoudid reveals that Tom, like her and everybody else in the world, has no real choice:

> she took him on her lap very kindly . . .and put him in mind how it was not her fault, because she was wound up inside, like watches, and could not help doing things whether she liked or not. And then she told him how he had been in the nursery long enough, and *must* go out now and see the world, if he intended ever to be a man; and how he *must* go all alone by himself, as every one else that ever was born has to go. (p145, italics mine)[12]

It is only through persuasion, warning and the knowledge that he really has no choice that Tom finally agrees to make his journey. He sets out as Mrs Bedonebyasyoudid gives him a final caution:

> You were very near being turned into a beast once or twice, little Tom. Indeed, if you had not made up your mind to go on this journey, and see the world, like an Englishman, I am not sure but that you would have ended as an eft in a pond. (p153)

At this admonition Tom declares: 'Oh, dear me! ...sooner than that, and be all over slime, I'll go this minute, if it is to the world's end' (p153). When he finally meets Mother Carey, she reveals that she helps 'make things make themselves' (p174). This paradox underpins the idea of forced action which dominates the narrative. For Kingsley, one must never believe in unadulterated choice, because choice will only ever lead to a life 'as an eft in a pond' (p153).

Kingsley was a known advocate of Darwin's evolutionary theory, but in crafting *The Water Babies* he limits evolutionary possibility and uses its ideas to force a social agenda. Because Tom undergoes a startling physical transformation, it would seem that evolution plays a key part in his moral development, but evolution, like free-will and heavenly influence, is shown to have a limited role in human development. Both free will and evolution lead to degeneration, and such degeneration is especially likely for those outside of England, or for the English lower orders. Those of the upper classes, like Ellie and her father, have no history or future need for change. In *The Water Babies*, position in life is fixed at birth, and if you are lucky enough to be a true Englishman, you will lead a good and productive life - providing you don't *choose* to deviate from your path.

Notes

1. This is a firmly established critical position mentioned in many publications concerning *The Water Babies*. However, examples of work that particularly focus on this aspect of *The Water Babies* include: Gillian Beer's *Darwin's Plot's* and 'Pebbles on the Shore', Colin Manlove's chapter on Kingsley in *Modern Fantasy: Five Studies*, Amanda Hodgson's article 'Defining the Species: Apes, Savages and Humans in Scientific and Literary Writing of the 1860's' and Arthur Johnston's article 'The Water Babies: Kingsley's Debt to Darwin'.

2. For a discussion of Kingsley's colonialism that does not consider how it relates to his use of evolution, see Jo-Ann Wallace, who argues: 'The intended middle-class, male, child reader - Kingsley's 'dear little man' - is clearly being prepared for *his* role in managing

less fully evolved Others, whether the working classes of his domestic environment or the native Others of the colonies' (Wallace, 1994: 180).

3. For a discussion of the relationship of sanitary reform to *The Water Babies* and a consideration of the baptismal connection of Tom's desire to be cleansed, see Brendon Rapple's essay 'The Motif of Water in Charles Kingsley's *The Water Babies*.' For more recent discussion of Kingsley's proto-environmentalism see Naomi Wood, 'A (Sea) Green Victorian.'

4. Colin Manlove also briefly mentions this racial connection: 'if the body is taken as the soul's expression of itself, then it becomes necessary to admit that one may tell a man's nature from his physiognomy [. . .].This contributed to his contempt for coloured races (something of this is behind the account of Tom's ugly black sweep's body in *The Water Babies*)' (Manlove, 1975: 40). Brian Street similarly points out that moral degeneration in *The Water Babies* leads to savagery (Street, 1975: 90-91). For a summary of Kingsley's racial politics, see Reginald Horsman, who argues that Kingsley 'believed that degenerate races [. . .] were better off dead' (Horsman, 1976: 410).

5. Amanda Hodgson particularly explores Tom's presentation as a 'black ape' in *The Water Babies*. She comments on the frequent satires in the text of the famous debate between Thomas Huxley and Richard Owen on whether ape brains contained the *hippocampus minor* and explores how Tom's position as both black man and beast relates to the Victorian need for a stable identity in the light of Darwinian theory: 'The mid-Victorian tendency to equate black races, races which they called savage, with apes relates to the concurrent attempt to understand the nature of humankind in historical, evolutionary terms.' (Hodgson, 1999: 240-241)

6. On the poor as a different biological 'race', see Nancy Stepan, 'Biology and Degeneration.' For an interesting link between the poor and racial others that was centred on chimneysweeps, see Tim Barringer, 'Images of Otherness and Visual Production of Difference.'

7. This is, of course, a definition Tolkien takes issue with in his famous essay on fairy tales. (Tolkien, 1997: 109-110)

8. Manlove also seems however to take this argument a step too far, claiming that 'the creatures of the book are all natural' (Manlove, 1975: 24). While the natural order is certainly represented strongly in the text, both the fairies and the water babies remain supernatural beings. Although they operate as allegories for divine intervention, and despite Kingsley's assertions that 'you must never talk about 'ain't' and 'can't' when you speak of this great wonderful world round you'(Kingsley, 1994: 46), readers are firmly reminded that the story is a fairy tale, and that they must rely on learning and experience above supernatural influence.

9. For an alternative view see John C. Hawley, who argues that Mrs Bedonebyasyoudid is 'Kingsley's metaphor for social, religious, and, in the implied dialogue with scientists, physical evolution [. . .]' (Hawley, 1989: 21)

10. Valentine Cunningham does note the unsatisfactory fairy-tale ending in Kingsley's refusal to allow a marriage between Tom and Ellie, although not in relation to a limited form of evolution: 'Why, for that matter, is Tom not allowed to marry Ellie? [. . .]. Visiting her on Sundays hardly seems the sort of reward his cleansing was set up to provide. Bourgeois reluctance to let the sweep have the princess overwhelms the story's ending'. (Cunningham, 1985: 141)

11. Another contributory factor to the Gairfowl's extinction is her refusal to marry her deceased sister's husband. Kingsley seems to present this idea as quite honourable, despite the consequences, and it appears to relate to his denial of marriage between the salmon and the trout or Tom and Ellie. Once again, Kingsley places social propriety over natural selection.

12. For a discussion of Mrs Bedonebyasyoudid as a machine, see Manlove, 'Charles Kingsley, H. G. Wells, and the Machine in Victorian Fiction'.

Bibliography

Alderson, Brian (1995) Introduction. In Kingsley, Charles *The Water Babies*. Oxford: Oxford University Press, (ppix-xxiv)

Barringer, Tim (1996) Images of Otherness and Visual Production of Difference: Race and Labour in Illustrated Texts, 1850-1865. In West, Shearer (ed.) *The Victorians and Race*. Aldershot: Scolar, (pp34-52)

Beer, Gillian (2000) *Darwin's Plots: Evolutionary Narrative In Darwin, George Eliot And Nineteenth-Century Fiction.* Cambridge: Cambridge University Press

Beer, Gillian (1975) Kingsley: Pebbles On The Shore. *The Listener.* Vol. 93. (Pp506-7)

Cunningham, Valentine (1985) Soiled Fairy: The Water Babies in its Time. *Essays in Criticism.* Vol. 35, no. 2. (pp121-148)

Darwin, Charles (2004) *The Descent of Man.* (1871). London; Penguin

Darwin, Charles (1968) *The Origin of Species.* (1859). Burrow, J.W. (ed.) Harmondsworth: Penguin Books

Johnston, Arthur (1959) The Water Babies: Kingsley's Debt to Darwin. *English.* Vol.12. (pp215-219)

Hanawalt, Mary Wheat (1937) Charles Kingsley and Science. *Studies in Philology.* Vol. 34. (pp589-611)

Hawley, John C (1989) The Water Babies as Catechetical Paradigm. *Children's Literature Association Quarterly.* Vol.14, no. 1. (pp19-21)

Hodgson, Amanda (1999) Defining the Species: Apes, Savages and Humans in Scientific and Literary Writing of the 1860s. *Journal of Victorian Culture.* Vol. 4, no. 2. (pp228-251)

Horsman, Reginald (1976) Origins of Racial Anglo-Saxonism in Great Britain before 1850. *Journal of the History of Ideas.* Vol. 37. (pp387-410)

Kingsley, Charles (1876) *His Letters and Memories of His Life.* Kingsley, Frances E. (ed.) 2 vols. London: Kegan Paul

Kingsley, Charles (1994) *The Water Babies.* (1863). Hertfordshire: Wordsworth Editions

Macdonald, George (1996) *The Princess and the Goblin.* (1872). London: Puffin Books

Manlove, Colin (1975) Charles Kingsley. In *Modern Fantasy: Five Studies.* Cambridge: Cambridge University Press, (pp13-54)

Manlove, Colin (1993) Charles Kingsley, H. G. Wells, and the Machine in *Victorian Fiction. Nineteenth Century Literature.* Vol. 48. (pp212-239)

Ostry, Elaine. (2003) Magical Growth and Moral Lessons; or, How the Conduct Book Informed Victorian and Edwardian Children's Fantasy. *The Lion and the Unicorn.* Vol. 27. (pp27-56)

Rapple, Brendon. (1993-1995) The Motif of Water in Charles Kingsley's The Water Babies. *University of Mississippi Studies in English.* Vols. XI-XII. (pp259-271)

Stepan, Nancy. (1985) Biology and Degeneration: Races and Proper Places. In Chamberlin, J.E. & Gilman, Sander L. (eds.) *Degeneration: The Dark Side of Progress.* New York: Columbia UP, (pp97-120)

Street, Brian (1975) Evolution and race in popular literature: hierarchy and racial theory. In *The Savage in Literature: Representations of 'Primitive' Society in English Fiction 1858-1920.* London: Routledge, (pp78-105)

Tolkien, J. R. R. (1997) On Fairy-Stories. In Tolkien, Christopher (ed.) *The Monsters and the Critics.* London: Harper Collins Publishers, (pp109-163)

Vance, Norman (2004) Kingsley, Charles (1819-1875). *Oxford Dictionary of National Biography.*
<http://www.oxforddnb.com/view/article/15617>.
Accessed on 28.09.2006

Wallace, Jo-Ann (1994) De-Scribing The Water Babies: The Child in Post-Colonial Theory. In Tiffin, Chris & Lawson, Alan (eds.) *De-Scribing Empire: Post-Colonialism and Textuality.* New York: Routledge, (pp171-184)

Wood, Naomi (1995) A (Sea) Green Victorian: Charles Kingsley and The Water-Babies. *The Lion and the Unicorn.* Vol. 19, no. 2. (pp233-252)

Fiction for all ages?: 'All-ages-literature' as a new trend in late modern Norwegian children's literature

Åse Marie Ommundsen

By defining all-ages-literature as literature written without any particular audience in mind, and aesthetic autonomy as a necessary criterion for literary excellence, the famous Norwegian author Jon Fosse advocates a form of all-ages-literature that actually might pose a threat to children's literature. All-ages-literature must be written with an audience in mind, as it must address both a child reader and an adult reader at the same time, and not the one at the expense of the other, but to know if all-ages-literature really is also for children, it is imperative to find out who the narrators address. Who are the implied readers? What knowledge is demanded to fill out the blanks in the text? Fiction for all ages simultaneously addresses both a child reader and an adult reader, it communicates sound, pictures and meaning in a multi-voiced interaction.

Aesthetic autonomy and non-literary literature

In 1997 the famous Norwegian author Jon Fosse launched the notion of all-ages-literature as being a quality marker of children's literature. To write quality literature for children, you have to write all-ages-literature, Fosse claimed in a provoking article. Books written for children, he maintained, could not be serious literature because adaptation makes a text non-literary. As he put it: 'The notion of children's literature implies a denial of the aesthetic autonomy which first and last establishes serious literature.' (my translation). Fosse excludes children's literature from being serious literature from the outset, as it is written for children. It can only be quality if it is not especially for children.

Jon Fosse's mixing of the notion of all-ages-literature with aesthetic autonomy as an aesthetic principle was provocative for Norwegian authors of children's literature. However, it did not stimulate further debate. Even now, the commonly used notion of fiction for all ages, or all-ages-literature as it is called in Norway, has not been sufficiently clarified. The problem about Fosse's use of the term is that he defines it as literature that is not written for a specific readership. To create art, he claims, an artist must write without any particular audience in mind. The notion of an autonomous aesthetic - in the Norwegian debate called 'autonomy aesthetics' - may serve as a productive principle for Fosse's own writing. But, because the notion of aesthetic autonomy excludes any serious consideration of children's literature, it does not work as a basis for a theory in children's literature. In this article I will discuss the notion of all-ages-literature, extricate it from Fosse's definition, and introduce my own definition. By dividing the Norwegian all-ages-literature into three different groups, I will argue for different ways the notion can be used - and ways it cannot be used.

Is it possible to talk about aesthetic autonomy in connection with children's literature? Fosse's principle clashes with one of the most commonly accepted definitions of children's literature: 'Children's literature is literature which is written and published for children.' (Weinreich, 2000: 33). There is literature which is difficult to categorize in terms of intended audience. From the very beginning of children's literature, there have been several examples of border-crossing literature which addresses a dual audience, encompassing both a child and adult readership at the same time. Mark Twain's *The Adventures of Huckleberry Finn* (1874) is an example of a canonized dual audience text intentionally written for children. According to Aidan Chambers (Chambers, 2006), Twain, with Huck Finn, initiated a shift from writing for someone to writing as artwork, thinking, 'I must tell it like it was', instead of writing another nostalgic childhood story. Twain made an alliance with Huck, so that even if it may look like an adult book, it is (also) for children. In the preface from 1876 Mark Twain wrote:

> Although my book is intended mainly for the entertainment of boys and girls, I hope it will not be shunned by men and women on that account, for part of my plan has been to try pleasantly to remind adults of what they once were themselves, and of how they felt and thought and talked, and what queer enterprises they sometimes engaged in. (p2)

Barbara Wall argues that the narrator-narratee relationship 'is the distinctive marker of a children's book'. (Wall, 1991: 9). She points out that 'this relationship has changed markedly in the last one hundred and fifty years', and suggests that there are three distinct ways in which writers address children in their stories. Firstly, they may write for a single audience, using single address. The narrators will then address child narratees, overtly or covertly, showing no consciousness that adults too might read the work: 'concern for children's interests dominates their stories'. (Wall 1991: 35) Secondly, they may write for a double audience, using double address. Their narrators will then address child narratees overtly and self-consciously, and will also address adults,

> either overtly, as the implied author's attention shifts away from the implied child reader to a different older audience, or covertly, as the narrator deliberately exploits the ignorance of the implied child reader and attempts to entertain an implied adult reader by making jokes which are funny primarily because children will not understand them." (p35)

Thirdly, they may write for a dual audience, using dual address. Their narrators address child narratees, usually covertly, but often openly

> either using the same 'tone of seriousness' which would be used to address adult narratees, or confidentially sharing the story in a way that allows adult narrator and child narratee a conjunction of interests. (p35)

Their stories are dominated by concern for something other than purely children's interests:

> pride in the artist's crafts, perhaps, or commitment to an idea; in the case of the greatest of all writers for children, the Charles Dodgson of the *Alice* books, a delight in language and logical problems." (p35)

Fiction for all?

Is it possible to address all ages at the same time? There are clearly huge differences in possible audiences of what we call children's literature, from picture books for very small children to borderline-literature for young adults. Young adult fiction is another type of borderline literature, but still something different from all-ages-literature. As adolescence is a borderline age, young adult fiction is often difficult to distinguish from the adult novel. The dual address disappears, and is replaced with a kind of single address.

There are also large individual differences among the human beings we define as children, as the term is used about people up to the age of 18. The complexity increases because readers within the same age group may also vary considerably when it comes to competence and literacy. Just as there are more and less competent child readers, the same is true of adult readers.

This said, I find fiction for all ages to be one of the main trends in late modern Norwegian children's literature. The trend can be seen as a result of changing conceptions of the child and of the adult, the adultification of childhood and childification of adulthood. (Ommundsen, 2006). Over the last few years several young Norwegian authors have had great success with their all-ages-literature, which can take several forms. It may be picture books for children bought and read by adults, such as *Snill* (*Kind*) (2002) by Gro Dahle and Svein Nyhus; or children's books that become cult bestsellers for adults, such as Erlend Loe's books about the truck driver Kurt (1994, 1995, 1998, 2003). On the other hand it may be picture books for adults read by children, such as Lars Elling's *To og To* (*Two by Two*) (1997); or it may be adult books that achieve cult status amongst both teenagers and adults, such as *Naiv. Super* (1996) by Erlend Loe. Sometimes booksellers are themselves marketing books for a dual audience, so that there will be two different versions of the same work on sale, one in the adult section, one in the children's. This was the case with Henrik Hovland's picture book about the alligator Johannes Jensen, *Johannes Jensen og kjærligheten* (*Johannes Jensen and Love*) (2005) which is sold in a large format for children, and a small format (mini-edition) for adults - launched as the perfect present for Valentine's Day. Another example is Bjørn Sortland's *12 ting som må gjerast rett før verda går under* (*12 Things Which Have To Be Done Just Before The World Goes Under*) (2001), a novel thematizing existential questions.

Copyright: Henrik Hovland/ill Torill Kove (2005). *Johannes Jensen og kjærligheten*. Oslo: Cappelen.
Copyright: Bjørn Sortland (2001). *12 ting som må gjerast før verda går under*. Oslo: Aschehoug.

The notion of all-ages-literature is increasingly used and sells well. However, though the term is quite marketable, it does not mean that all the texts actually address all readers. In fact, it is quite easy to find examples of so-called all-ages-literature which do not address the child reader at all. Thus I will argue that to be fiction for all ages, it must provide reader positions for both a child reader and an adult reader, and address what Barbara Wall calls a dual audience. To give the term 'all-ages-literature' more conceptual clarity, I offer the following definition:

> All-ages-literature is a kind of literature which addresses both a child reader and an adult reader at the same time, and not the one at the expense of the other. (Ommundsen 2006).

According to Wall, dual address is rare and difficult:

> Dual address, which might be found at any time, is rare and difficult, presupposing as it does that a child narratee is addressed and an adult reader simultaneously satisfied. Works which draw a dual audience in spite of being addressed to children, however, are not so rare. (Wall, 1991: 35-36)

However, though not a new phenomenon, there is no doubt that fiction for all ages has been sharply on the rise in recent years. Sandra Beckett became aware of 'the fact that the 'shifting boundaries between children's and adult literature' constituted a significant international trend in contemporary literature', which resulted in one of the few books written on the matter, *Transcending Boundaries. Writing for a Dual Audience of Children and Adults* (1999). As Beckett points out, 'The latter half of the twentieth century has been a particularly productive period for dual-audience texts, a trend that seems to be sharply on the rise in recent years.' (Beckett, 1999: xiii). I think the English terms 'dual-audience text', 'fiction with dual readerships', and 'crossover literature', are not necessarily used about the same phenomenon. Perhaps because of the lack of a precise definition, Beckett actually refers to the Norwegian term 'allalderslitteratur', all-ages-literature, or simply uses 'literature for all ages' in the discussion of contemporary children's fiction that 'attempts to speak to the child and the adult simultaneously and on equal terms in what Barbara Wall calls dual address'. (Beckett, 1999: xiv)

However, Norwegian fiction for all ages may be many things. I have chosen to divide the different kinds of fiction for all ages into three main groups, as discussed below.

Different kinds of fiction for all ages

Because all-ages-literature can include very different kinds of literature, from that which exhibits naïve simplicity on the one hand, to a complex multivoicedness on the other, I have categorized it into three different types: naivistic, existential, and complex - although, in practice, these terms sometimes overlap. To understand the three different types, it may be fruitful to imagine them as three different ways of approaching the world, using three different ways of looking.

Naivistic all-ages-literature: the childly gaze

From the 1990s there was a naivistic turn in contemporary Norwegian literature. In naivistic all-ages-literature the world is seen through the eyes of a child or a childly adult. I here use childly as a positive concept, as argued in Peter Hollindale's *Signs of Childness in Children's Books* (1997). Naivistic all-ages-literature is often humorous, as in the most obvious example, Erlend Loe's books about the truck driver Kurt. Erlend Loe may be said to have initiated the trend to write naivistic all-ages-literature with his books about Kurt. The main character Kurt is a childly adult who in the first book, together with his wife and three children, experiences exciting adventures travelling around the world on a big fish. (*Fisken* (*The Fish*) 1994). But Kurt's life is not always easy, and in the following books he struggles with problems like greed, in *Kurt blir grusom* (*Kurt Becomes Cruel*) (1995), and jealousy in *Kurt koker hodet* (*Kurt Boils his Head*) (2003). In *Kurt quo vadis?* (1998) Kurt feels like a failure. Being the only truck driver in a party with architects, teachers and doctors, Kurt decides to find something more important to do with his life. He wants to increase his status and become famous. Kurt's feelings are easy to recognize for the adult reader, and show, in Wall's words, a 'concern for something other than purely children's interests' (Wall, 1991: 35). When Loe wrote the first book about Kurt (1994), it was the publisher who suggested it could be a children's book, with the author himself claiming not to have known what he had written. As Beckett points out, a denial of the distinction between children's and adult's literature can be seen as an escape from the stigma of children's literature:

> Dual-audience authors whose children's books have gained them an international reputation and handsome profits often deny their position as a children's author, or the child addressee of their texts, or even that there is a distinction between children's and adult literature, determined, it would seem, not to allow themselves to be labeled as "children's authors". (Beckett, 1999: xvii)

But Loe's books for children and his adult novels are actually all written in the same naïve tone, where complicated things are simplified. His books share the simplicity of language, the sophisticated naïvism, the humour, the distanced irony and a number of motifs, like the motif of a father separated from his regular family life, or the idea of one animal corpse providing food and lasting for a year without storing, found both in the books about Kurt and in the adult novel *Doppler* (2004). Thus it may be difficult to distinguish between his children's and adults' books, a point that has also been raised by the critics. For instance, reviews of his picture book *Maria og José (Maria and José)* (1994) differ greatly dependent on whether the critic has read it as a children's book or as a picture book for adults.

Erlend Loe/ill Kim Hjorthøy. (1998) *Kurt for alle.* Oslo: Cappelen.
Erlend Loe/ill Kim Hjorthøy. (1998) *Kurt quo vadis?* Oslo: Cappelen.

Existential all-ages-literature: the wondering gaze

Since Jostein Gaarder wrote his bestseller *Sofies verden, (Sophie's World)* (1995) there has been a strong tendency to publish more philosophical all-ages books which thematically deal with existential questions common in all human life. As Loe can be said to have initiated the naivistic trend, Gaarder can be said to have initiated the existential trend in Norwegian literature. In existential all-ages-literature, the wondering gaze, where the questions are more important than the answers, marks a shift from the earlier, didactic children's literature. Even if we may find examples of all-ages-literature which is both existential and naivistic at the same time, this need not be a defining characteristic. Existential all-ages-literature focuses on existential questions both children and adults have in common. The picturebook *Verden har ingen hjørner* (*The World Has No Corners*) (1999) by Svein Nyhus is one example. It is a philosophical and poetic book where Viktor's wondering gaze at who we are, where we come from and where we are going, in Wall's words, 'allows adult narrator and child narratee a conjunction of interests' (Wall, 1991: 35). The boy's wondering gaze is found both in the text and in Viktor's big eyes in the illustrations. The illustrations extend and play with the existential approaches of the text, like the following two examples (my translation):

3.
Bread is only crumbs
And waves are only drops.
I am also put together
by many tiny bits.
But my skin
keeps it all in place.

12.
I am more than just I.
I am a carrier.
For even if I take off all my clothes,
I carry some soil under my nails
and food in my tummy,
and in my hair there is a small twig.

Svein Nyhus. 1999. *Verden har ingen hjørner.* Oslo: Gyldendal Tiden.

The written text in *Verden har ingen hjørner* is not a traditional narrative story, but a sequence of scattered ideas, going through the mind of a little boy. It can be read as continuous text or even disconnected - as starting points for a philosophical dialogue between child and adult. The narrative elements, like Viktor's movement in time and place, are only expressed in the illustrations. As the illustrations tell different stories, while the written text can be read as if Viktor stays in a box throughout the book, reading the written text without the illustrations - or vice versa - can create completely different experiences. Svein Nyhus has made two more picture books, *Jeg!* (*I!*) (2004) and *Ingen* (*Nobody*) (2002), which also would fit into the existential category. He is also the illustrator of some great picture books by Gro Dahle, like *Snill* (*Kind*), which would fit into the next category.

Complex all-ages-literature: the advanced gaze

The distinctive character of the border-crossing children's literature can thus be attributed to quite different characteristics: naïve simplicity on the one hand, which may be characterised as a kind of minimalism, but it can also be the opposite: extensive, complex, full of details and multi-levelled text structures. Maria Nikolajeva (1996) claims that children's literature comes of age, or grows up. And by the metaphor of growing up she means something positive, that it grows more literary, and achieves higher quality. With Bakhtin's notion of 'polyphony', she shows how children's literature has developed from traditional epic structures to new polyphonic structures: 'The polyphony, or "multivoicedness" of modern children's novels, is manifested through a new type of narrator, in the palimpsestic multilevel text structure, in various experimental forms and advanced narrative techniques.' (Nikolajeva, 1996: 9).

Complex all-ages-literature, with its advanced, polyphonic structures, demands a competent reader. Picture books as complex all-ages-literature are especially interesting due to the fact that they address smaller children who themselves can not read the text. On the other hand, small children may be very good at reading the details in the pictures. Thus complex picture books for smaller children presuppose an interaction between child and adult in the reading act, as picture books of course are most often shared in a reading context marked by physical closeness between child and adult. One example of complex all-ages-literature is *Krusedullen* (*Doodles*) (2005) by Simon Stranger and Eivind Gulliksen. This is a picture book for small children with polyphony, intertextuality, metafiction and a mixing of genres. *Krusedullen* is a story about Doodles who came to life in a rush, scribbled down by the illustrator Eivind Gulliksen, who himself is a character in the story - playing the role as an illustrator and the creator of the Doodles. Doodles gets his own television show and becomes famous, but ends up experiencing an identity crisis, feeling empty. The illustrations expand and challenge the written text, and also tell their own stories. The polyphony of the book challenges the reader to make her own choice as to whom to believe, and to become a co-creator of the story through the reading process. There are lots of intertextual references, some of them only well known to the adult reader who watches television late at night, like caricatures of famous personalities from Norwegian broadcasting. But the caricatures are also humorous in themselves, and do not necessarily need to be recognized to create the desired comic effect.

Another example of a complex all-ages picture book is *Frosken (The Frog)* (2003) by Hans Sande and Gry Moursund, although it could be argued that this book also falls into the existential category, as it is asking existential questions and criticizing religion through its two parallel stories.

Hans Sande/ill Gry Moursund. 2003. *Frosken*. Oslo: Gyldendal.Simon Stranger/ill Eivind Gulliksen. 2005. *Krusedullen*. Oslo: Damm.

Fiction for no one?

It is also easy to find examples of literature, presented as all-ages-literature, which do not address the child reader at all. Like Umberto Eco, we can look for the concept of 'openness' and the model reader (implied reader) to see if a given text offers a reader position to the child reader. Zohar Shavit asks of the new, so-called all-ages-literature, what happens if the child reader is ignored? In *The Double Attribution of Texts for Children and How It Affects Writing for Children* (1999) she writes:

> Adults always will remain involved in the writing for children, but they must remember that children's literature is, after all, written not for them, but for children. Like a doting father who buys himself an electric train in order to fulfill his own childhood dream that never came true, more and more recent books for children seem intent on satisfying adult wishes and, in this sense, often appeal to adults at the expense of the child-reader. (Shavit, 1999: 95)

Some works are not really for all ages at all. One example of a book presented as all-ages-literature which I rather would define as a picture book for adults, is the prizewinning *Zoo logisk (Zoo (So) Logical)* (2005). This book consists of solid prose, and is rather heavy at that, full of references the child reader has no possibility of understanding. It resembles an animal encyclopaedia, playing with the well-known genre of animal books for children. The presented animals are very unusual, as the illustrations are made out of things which might look like an animal or a fantasy-animal. The giraffe is for instance a measuring tape, and a safety pin is presented as another animal. This is of course a play on words, as the Norwegian word for safety pin, 'sikkerhetsnål', ends with 'ål' which is a fish (eel). *Zoo logisk* contains difficult language, difficult terminology and intertextual references unknown to children. The problem with calling this book all-ages-literature increases due to the fact that a great part of the humour is dependent on these references which are only accessible for adults.

In an intermediate position I place the picture book *Fokus på ku (Focus on Cow)* (2004). Playing both with the tradition of animal books and fact books, it focuses on cows through humour and wordplay, especially play with homonyms. This is also a book full of intertextual references the child reader is unlikely to be familiar with, often placed as small details in the pictures. We can, for instance, find a red book looking like The Laws of Norway: Norges Lover, but here the book is called Norges Låver, which means the barns of Norway. This is a play with homonymous words, as the words for laws and barns in Norwegian are homonyms. On the wall we can find posters of both Julio Iglesias, called Kulio Iglesias (ku is the Norwegian word for cow), an artist probably only recognized by adults, and Madonna, who is called Mødonna, mø being the Norwegian word for cows' typical 'moo' sound. Madonna will probably be well-known to at least the older children. But at the same time *Fokus På Ku* has humour at other, more accessible levels, even for small children, like for example 'When cows poop, they always try to make it look like cinnamon-rolls', a fact which also can be seen in the picture.

Ragnar Aalbu. 2004. *Focus on cow*. Oslo: Cappelen.

Something more

Recently, various types of fiction for all ages have constituted a main trend in children's literature in Norway. Money is one possible explanation. Picture books for children get picture book support, which picture books for adults do not. There is also the obvious fact that adults choose books for children. Another possible explanation is the increased status that writing and publishing all-ages-literature gives, compared to the traditional low status of children's literature. Using Bourdieu's theories, we can point out the field of children's literature's shared wish to increase the status and prestige of children's literature.

Nikolajeva's coming-of-age theory is another possible explanation, as is children's increased competence as readers (literacy), living in a globalized late modern society. The changed relationship between child and adult, and the adultification of childhood and childification of adulthood, is mirrored in literature in a two-way movement (Ommundsen, 2006).

Through my discussion of the commonly used notion of all-ages-literature, I hope to have provided a better definition to replace the one launched by Jon Fosse in 1997. By defining all-ages-literature as literature written without any particular audience in mind, and aesthetic autonomy as a necessary criterion for literary excellence, he advocates a form of all-ages-literature that actually might pose a threat to children's literature. It is easy to find examples of literature presented as all-ages-literature which do not address the child reader at all. According to my definition, all-ages-literature must indeed be written with an audience in mind, as it must address both a child reader and an adult reader at the same time, and not the one at the expense of the other. To know if all-ages-literature really is also for children, it is imperative to find out who the narrators address. Who are the implied readers? What knowledge is demanded to fill out the blanks in the text?

The ambivalent status of children's literature demands of adults working in the field a recognition that the reader in the text has to be a child. Literature which presupposes an adult's pre-understanding is adult literature. Of course, there is nothing wrong with adult literature as such. But fiction for all ages is something more: simultaneously addressing both a child reader and an adult reader, it communicates sound, pictures and meaning in a multi-voiced interaction.

Bibliography

Bakhtin, Michail (1963) *Dostojevskijs poetik.* Gråbo: Anthropos.

Beckett, Sandra (ed). (1999) *Transcending Boundaries. Writing for a Dual Audience of Children and Adults.* New York & London: Garland Publishing Inc.

Bourdieu, Pierre (1979) *Distinksjonen. En sosiologisk kritikk av dømmekraften.* Oslo: Pax Forlag

Chambers, Aidan (2006) Crossing Boundaries: The Youth Novel as the Story of Creative Transgression. Guest Lecture at University of Oslo 6.4.2006

Eco, Umberto (1989) *The Open Work*. Cambridge, Massachusetts: Harvard University Press

Fosse, Jon (1998) All-alder-litteratur in: *Årboka 1998. Litteratur for barn og unge.* Oslo: Det Norske Samlaget

Hollindale, Peter (1997) *Signs of Childness in Children's Books*. Stroud: The Thimble Press

Iser, Wolfgang (1978) *The Act of Reading. A Theory of Aesthetic Response.* Baltimore: John Hopkins University Press

Kampp, Bodil (2002) *Barnet og den voksne i det børnelitterære rum.* København: Danmarks Pædagogiske Universitet

Nikolajeva, Maria (1996) *Children's Literature Comes of Age: Toward a New Aesthetic.* New York: Garland

Ommundsen, Åse Marie (2004) Girl Stuck in the Wall: Narrative Changes in Norwegian Children's Literature Exemplified by the Picture Book *Snill*. In: *Bookbird*. 2004: 42 (1), 24-26

Ommundsen, Åse Marie (2006) Barndom i senmoderniteten (Childhood in the late modern age) In: *Årboka 2006. Litteratur for barn og unge.* Oslo: Samlaget

Ommundsen, Åse Marie (2006) *All-alder-litteratur - Litteratur for alle eller Ingen?* (All-ages-literature. Literature for all or no one?) Oslo: Pax

Shavit, Zohar (1999) The Double Attribution of Texts for Children and How It Affects Writing for Children. In: Beckett, Sandra (ed) 1999. *Transcending Boundaries. Writing for a Dual Audience of Children and Adults.* New York & London: Garland Publishing Inc.

Tønnessen, Elise Seip (2000) *Barns møte med TV. Tekst og tolkning i en ny medietid.* Oslo: Universitetsforlaget

Twain, Mark (1992; 1876) *Tom Sawyer and Huckleberry Finn.* Hertfordshire: Wordsworth

Wall, Barbara (1991) *The Narrator's Voice. The Dilemma of Children's Fiction.* Basingstoke: Macmillan

Weinreich, Torben (2000) *Children's Literature - Art or Pedagogy?* Frederiksberg: Roskilde University Press

Colonialism and War in Children's Literature: Korea 1935-1953

Sarah Park

Literature by and about Koreans and Korean Americans set in colonial Korea and the Korean War has been growing steadily for the past decade, but it could present more nuanced images if there was more diversity in the storylines and portrayal of the politics of the time. In anticipation of the continual growth of this genre, parents and educators should consider the benefits of sharing these particular voices with children as a starting point to talk about trauma, war, colonialism and reconciliation.

In the summer of 2000 I flew to the Republic of Korea to visit my grandparents, and my trip coincided with the fifty-year anniversary of the beginning of the Korean War. A major part of the commemoration was the highly televised reunification of 100 families between the Republic of Korea (South Korea) and the Democratic People's Republic of Korea (North Korea). It was the first time that I, a third generation Korean American, witnessed the real ramifications of that devastating time period. My parents, born one year after the 1953 ceasefire, never spoke of it. Neither did my grandparents.

My family's silence about this topic mirrors the silences in children's literature. Since the 1990s, children's books published in the United States have started to address war, trauma and violence in larger numbers than ever before (Baer, 2000; Bat-Ami, 1994; Galbraith, 2000; Harada, 1998; Hollindale, 1997; Kertzer, 1999; Kidd, 2005; Myers, 2000; Smith, 2005; Walter, 2000). The majority of these stories are set during the two World Wars, many on the subject of the Holocaust. Stories set in colonial Korea and the Korean War have been relatively few. Fortunately, several Korean American authors are beginning to share their family stories.

The Korean peninsula endured colonialism, war, political and social upheavals, and economic crises throughout the twentieth century. However, since the 1970s, the Republic of Korea has participated actively in the global economy and been internationally recognized for producing award-winning books and films. While we should celebrate these accomplishments, it is crucial to learn about the past - both the negative and the positive. Regarding the mission of the Auschwitz Museum, Poland Prime Minister Jerzy Buzek said 'working together to preserve for posterity the tragic heritage of the Nazi policy... will serve the cause of reconciliation and mutual understanding.' In the same way, the legacies of Japanese colonialism and the Korean War must be preserved for posterity and the purpose of reconciliation.

Modern Korean history

Korea was historically labelled as the 'Hermit Kingdom' for her strong isolationist policies (Eckert et al 1991: 194), but corruption and factionalism within the political leadership at the beginning of the twentieth century created a power vacuum for the Japanese government to take advantage and occupy the country. Despite aggressive Korean resistance, Japan officially annexed and occupied Korea from 1910 to 1945. Appeals for help to foreign countries fell on deaf ears. On March 1, 1919, Korean nationalists organised a peaceful demonstration declaring the independence of Korea and calling for the Japanese to leave the peninsula. The Japanese responded by shooting into crowds and beating demonstrators; thousands of Korean nationalists, both male and female, were imprisoned and killed.

Japan attempted to eradicate all aspects of Korean culture and tradition. Koreans were forbidden to speak their native language and forced to adopt Japanese names. Korean students learned Japanese history in their classrooms. Many worked in rice farming, which was exported to Japan. Leftover food was rationed to Korean families; rations increased with obedience to the Japanese Empire, or decreased with resistance. Opposition to Japanese rule often met with imprisonment, physical torture, or death. Tens of thousands of Koreans perished at the hands of the Japanese.

Korea was liberated from Japan in 1945 with the Imperial Army's defeat in World War II. However, the former Soviet Union and the United States arbitrarily divided the peninsula along an invisible line at the thirty-eighth parallel. Unable to agree on how to govern a suddenly liberated country, they held separate elections for a Korean president. On June 25, 1950, the Democratic People's Republic of Korea (North Korea) attacked the Republic of Korea (South Korea), instigating a three year war that left the peninsula - and its families - further divided (Cumings, 1997; Cumings, 2004; Eckert et al, 1991; Oberdorfer, 1997).

Korean diaspora

In 1903, Koreans began immigrating systematically to Hawaii to work on sugar plantations (Takaki, 1998: 55-56). However, Japan stopped Korean emigration when it occupied the country and thus few Koreans emigrated after 1905 (p57). In 1952, a small but significantly growing number of Korean War orphans and war brides began to immigrate to the United States (Yuh, 2002). In 1965 the Immigration and Naturalization Services Act abolished the previously restrictive national origins quota, opening the gates to thousands of Korean immigrants. There are now more than one million Koreans living in the United States, and approximately half of the population was born in the United States and is under the age of eighteen (United States Census, 2000), yet the first few children's books about Koreans and Korean Americans were not written from within the community[1]. The recent growth of self-written Korean American literature is part of a larger phenomenon of ethnic peoples telling their own stories.

Social relevance

Many children's literature scholars advocate publishing stories that include culturally specific perspectives (Cai, 2002; Hade, 1997; Henderson and May, 2005; Larrick, 1965; Nodelman and Reimer, 2003; Rochman, 1993; Sims, 1982; Sims Bishop, 1994; Yokota, 1993). Culturally specific children's literature is important because

> ...children need literature that serves as a window onto lives and experiences different from their own, *and* literature that serves as a mirror reflecting themselves and their cultural values, attitudes, and behaviors (Sims Bishop, 1994: xiv).

Literature is also educational; it can be an 'effective way for children to learn about the diversity within and among cultures and to gain a sense of a country's ethnic history' (Harada, 1998: 19). For all readers, literature serves to expose issues of 'human rights and problems of ethnic identity' (p21).

Educators may hesitate to expose children to depictions of oppressive governments and violence in books, but it is imperative for children to read about injustices on both local and international scales. Kenneth Kidd argues that 'we no longer have the luxury of denying the existence or postponing the child's confrontation with evil' (Kidd, 2005: 121). In a generation where children can watch two planes crash into the World Trade Centre and see soldiers and civilians dying in Afghanistan and Iraq on television, adults have the responsibility of talking about war and violence with children to help them grow up to be knowledgeable and participative agents in their local, national and global communities.

When adults are silent on a controversial topic, be it war, abortion, or racism, children will also learn to be silent. This can lead to a deficiency in critical thinking skills which, in turn, can contribute to the lack of a

117

responsive and active community which is politically astute (Bat-Ami, 1994: 86). Engaging children in the reading process as active learners as opposed to passive listeners makes them more likely to grow up to be 'future peacemakers' (p88). This is especially important for Korean Americans whose parents and grandparents survived experiences of colonialism and war. Reading their stories can help children understand their elders and participate in healing processes with them.

Trauma theory

Literature is testimony of trauma, and trauma needs to be expressed by one person to another (Kidd, 2005: 124). That is, in the same way that Lois Lowry's *The Giver* (1993) shares his memories with Jonas and thus is relieved of pain, survivors of traumatic events need to share their experiences with others in order to start the process of healing. Katherine Capshaw Smith states that 'individual trauma constitutes social trauma, and through storytelling we render traumatic experiences sensible - and, of course, we also reflect on its final insensibility' (Smith, 2005: 118). In the introduction to *The Day our World Changed: Children's Art of 9/11* (2002), Dr Harold Koplewicz cautions that how the children of September 11 'handle this new sense of vulnerability, and... how we as adults help them find their way, will have a tremendous influence on our country's future' (Goodman, 2002). If, as Santayana suggests, 'Those who cannot remember the past are destined to repeat it,' it then follows that one must *know* the past in order to remember it.

Research addressing trauma and violence in children's literature became more common in the 1990s. Representations of the Holocaust are particularly visible; studies of these children's books provide useful frameworks with which to explore similar themes in Japanese occupation and Korean War literature. However, a bibliographic search confirms the paucity of children's books about Japanese colonialism (1910-1945) and the Korean War (1950-1953), particularly those written by Korean Americans and from the perspective of Korean youth. In this paper, I examine children's books set in these two traumatic periods in order to excavate recurring motifs and identify limitations, and analyse their meaning and significance in relation to the ways in which they portray the complexities and tragedies of early modern Korean history.

Literature about Japanese colonialism and the Korean War

The six stories in this study take place between 1935 and 1953, recounting the transitions through the last decade of colonialism, Korea's liberation from Japan, and the Korean War. They are all written by Korean Americans who either lived through this period, or are descendants of those who survived.

Folklorist Barre Toelken claims that 'taken one by one, the stories do not provide much historical data, while taken together they provide a rich kaleidoscope' (Toelken, 1996: 404). Holocaust scholar Elizabeth Baer states, 'no one book is sufficient unto itself as a confrontation; that is, a child would need to read several texts to begin to grasp the reality of the Holocaust' (Baer, 2000: 386). The same applies to stories about colonised and war torn Korea. Multiple stories, therefore, should provide richer material to present a nuanced portrait of Korean children's experiences of Japanese occupation and the Korean War.

This paper explores three middle grade novels; *Year of Impossible Goodbyes* (Choi, 1991), *Echoes of the White Giraffe* (Choi, 1993), and *When My Name was Keoko* (Park, 2002). In *Year of Impossible Goodbyes*, which is largely autobiographical, Sookan's mother runs a sock factory for the Japanese while the men are away at labour camps or working for the independence movement. The sequel, *Echoes of the White Giraffe*, follows Sookan, her mother and younger brother as they take refuge in Pusan until the end of the Korean War. In *When My Name was Keoko*, the alternating voices of Sun-hee and her older brother Tae-yul weave together vignettes which the author heard from her elders about growing up in the last few years of Japanese colonialism.

Three picture books are discussed; *Peacebound Trains* (Balgassi, 1996), *My Freedom Trip: a Child's Escape from North Korea* (Park and Park, 1998) and *Halmoni's Day* (Bercaw, 2000). *Peacebound Trains* frames a story about the Korean War within a contemporary narrative about a Korean American girl (Sumi) and her grandmother living in the United States. *My Freedom Trip* tells the terrifying journey of one young girl's escape from North Korea. The protagonist, Soo, is Frances Park's and Ginger Park's real life mother. Finally, *Halmoni's Day* relates the relationship between Korean American Jennifer and her *Halmoni* (grandmother), who is visiting from Korea. This picture book also frames a story within a story; *Halmoni* tells Jennifer's classmates about the Korean War's effects on her family during her childhood.

Within these books, several recurring motifs signify what the authors choose to share with children about living through Japanese colonialism and the Korean War.

Separation of family

Family separation is the most ubiquitous motif among all of the stories. Each story includes at least one major family member who is separated or lost during the Japanese occupation or the Korean War, and their absences are acutely painful for the protagonists. For example, at the beginning of *Year of Impossible Goodbyes*, all the older men in Sookan's family are absent. At the end, Sookan and Inchun flee south to find them, but they lose their mother along the way. In the sequel, Sookan, Inchun and their mother are again separated from the older men, who are this time absent because of the Korean War. Sookan wonders, 'We hadn't heard a thing since our separation from them. Were they still alive?' (p4).

Also, in *When My Name was Keoko*, Tae-yul tells his parents,' "I enlisted in the Imperial Army... If I join the army, things will be much better for you... I need to help the family the best way I can." His mother's response, "What help will you be to us if you die?" '(pp113-114) reflects the anxiety and anguish felt by Korean mothers who helplessly watched their sons serve in the Japanese army during World War II.

Peacebound Trains, *Halmoni's Day* and *My Freedom Trip* are about parents, husbands or wives being left behind during the outbreak of the Korean War. At the end of *My Freedom Trip*, Soo says, ' "I never saw my mother again. How could we have known that the river I crossed would separate us forever?" ' These stories bear witness to how the Japanese occupation and Korean War affected and disrupted all Korean families.

Fleeing south

Related to the first motif, fleeing southward occurs in almost all of the stories. Sumi's grandmother takes refuge in Pusan, a city located in the southernmost tip of the Korean peninsula. A stranger asks Sookan and Inchun, ' "Did you lose someone trying to go south?" '(Choi, 1991: 141). Later an old man tells them, ' "Once you are on the other side of the fence, you will be in the South and you will be free" ' (p156); thus the South is associated with democracy. In the sequel, Sookan says, '"The war broke out in Seoul and we couldn't help it. We had no choice but to flee south to Pusan" '(Choi, 1993: 3). Soo also flees south from North Korea in pursuit of safety and democracy. It is crucial for children to understand these geographical and political separations in light of the continued division of both nations and families, as well as the peace talks and family reunification efforts that have taken place between the two countries since the year 2000.

Grandparents

The role of grandparents is also a critical motif. In a previous study of Korean American children in school stories, I explored how grandparents play the primary role in transmitting Korean culture to their Americanized grandchildren after moving to the United States (Park, 2004: 3). Similarly, four stories in this study portray a grandparent (or grandparent figure, such as the poet in *Echoes of the White Giraffe*) who passes the cultural heritage on to his or her grandchild. Sookan tells the reader, ' "I wasn't supposed to be learning any of the Korean...that Grandfather was teaching me" ' (p4). Understanding the function of grandparents in transmitting the Korean heritage to their grandchildren is imperative. It teaches children about the role of elders in the country where their parents and grandparents grew up, and helps them to understand that the country and its history are not unrelated to who they are today.

Authors' personal connections

Each of the books is a memoir or fictionalised family history, and thus the authors explain how occupation and war experiences powerfully shaped their lives. These explanations range from paragraphs on book jackets to long epilogues describing research and personal connections. The authors testify to how their family histories impact who they are today, and how their journeys to this place started long before they were born. Frances Park and Ginger Park tell 'a story based on their own mother's 'freedom trip' across the 38th parallel just prior to the outbreak of the Korean War.' (Park & Park, 1998) Reading these passages can show children the continuity and connectedness of the past to the present, and may encourage them to critically examine how their own lives fit into a larger history.

Female protagonists and authors

All of the stories are predominantly told from the female perspective. Sun-hee and her brother Tae-yul tell the story in alternating voices in *When My Name was Keoko*, but Sun-hee is the primary storyteller. She starts the story: ' "I wasn't supposed to listen to men's business, but I couldn't help it" ' (p1). Sookan says, ' "Because I was a girl, I was supposed to stay with the women" ' (p11). Worse, Korean girls were vulnerable to a fate that men were not; Sookan relates an incident where she is 'terribly afraid for the sock girls' because she hears her mother and aunt talking about 'spirit girls' being 'locked in latrines and used by [Japanese] soldiers' (p56). These girls are not supposed to know 'men's business' about their country's political situation, but they live this nightmare, and thus they have stories to tell, and wounds to heal.

Additionally, all of the stories are authored by Korean American women. In portraying women, the authors present the lives of those doubly oppressed by both their nationhood and gender. In writing their stories, the authors liberate and empower women, reclaiming their ethnic voices and breaking through the representative male voice that so often speaks for the Korean female in a traditionally patrilineal society.

Limitations

Elizabeth Baer suggests four criteria to measure the 'effectiveness and usefulness' (Baer, 2000: 384) of literature about the Holocaust. Modelled directly on her criteria, the six books in this study should:

Directly address the oppressive nature of Japanese colonialism and/or the harsh realities of the Korean War.
Present Japanese colonialism and the Korean War in their proper contexts of complexity, even when raising questions that cannot be answered.
Demonstrate the dangers associated with the effects of misdirected nationalism, oppression, violence, lack of democracy, colonialism, and worst of all, complacency.
Encourage readers to create a memory and social consciousness regarding prejudice, hatred and discrimination, and provide them with a framework to respond to the story.

While these children's books do begin to address the aforementioned points, there is still room for growth. Collectively these stories have three major limitations. The first is an active distancing from the depiction of death. For example, in the epilogue of *Year of Impossible Goodbyes*, Choi reports that cousin Kisa and Aunt Tiger, who are major characters, 'were shot with machine guns' (p169). Readers meet Sookan's father briefly at the end of the first novel, and she informs the reader at the end of the sequel that his 'name was on a list of men who had died' (p103). In both situations, Choi reports but does not show death. The reader gets to know Tae-yul intimately in *When My Name was Keoko* because he and his sister take turns narrating the story in the first person. Near the end, Sun-hee tells the reader, 'Tae-yul had flown his mission' and died as a kamikaze pilot (p165). However, three months later she says she sees 'Tae-yul, coming out the back door' (p180). He has *not* died. Tae-yul explains, 'I apologize to my family,... I realized you'd have gotten that last letter - that you all thought I was dead' (p183). Park apologizes through Tae-yul's character for deceiving the reader. She uses this twist to teach readers that death is something that happens to *other* people, that death is something that happens to the *other* kamikaze pilots, but not to Tae-yul.

Despite the fact that some of the books involve United States citizens and American settings, a second limitation of the texts is the conspicuous absence of a critique of the United States' silence during the colonial era up to 1945. Sun-hee explains that 'American forces had landed in Korea to help supervise the handover of the government' (p171), but does not complain about their absence during the oppressive colonial period. To Sun-hee, Americans are there to keep order and pass out chocolate (p175). Furthermore, the narratives taking place after 1945 do not assess critically the *very active* role the United States played in partitioning the country post-liberation. Nor do they scrutinise how the United States used the political turmoil in Korea to militarise the Cold War, and then maintain (and continues to maintain) it for its own project against Communism and North Korea. Instead, Sookan gushes,

> "I often wonder what Americans think about a small country like Korea. Our peninsula is so tiny and yet it is constantly being occupied or fought over... I don't understand how history and politics work, and maybe if I study in America, I will understand better" (p65).

In *Peacebound Trains*, Sumi's grandmother says the eyes of the American soldiers 'sparkled and swirled' like marbles (p29). While the picture books are written by second generation Korean Americans whose parents had immigrated to the United States and therefore may have chosen not to criticise their adopted country for its role in shaping Korea's future, the novels have more space to explore this issue, but they are also silent.

Finally, the identification of major motifs such as the role of grandparents and the almost universal female protagonists speaks to the lack of diversity among these stories. They vary somewhat aesthetically, but all frame similar storylines. This begs the question, is there only one Japanese occupation experience? Is there only one Korean War experience? Why do stories always begin near the end of the colonial era? Why are there no stories about the March 1, 1919 independence movement? How did boys of all ages live, especially since they were potential soldiers? What were other people's experiences? These questions point to the need for more stories and more scholarship.

Conclusion

These stories take place during colonialism and war, but they could present more nuanced images if there was more diversity in the storylines and portrayal of the politics that frame the time period in question. Literature by and about Koreans and Korean Americans has been growing steadily for the past decade, and will probably continue to grow as more Korean Americans explore their histories, ethnic heritage and identities. In anticipation of the continual growth of this genre, parents and educators should consider the benefits of sharing these particular voices with children as a starting point to talk about trauma, war and colonialism.

Note

1. *Tales Told in Korea* (1932) by Berta Metzger may be the earliest Korean folktale collection published in the United States, predating Frances Carpenter's more commonly known *Tales of a Korean Grandmother* (1947).

Bibliography

Baer, Elizabeth R. (2000) A New Algorithm in Evil: Children's Literature in a Post-Holocaust World. *The Lion and the Unicorn.* Vol. 24, no. 3. (pp378-401)

Balgassi, Haemi. Illustrated by Chris Soentpiet (1996) *Peacebound Trains.* New York: Clarion Books

Bat-Ami, Miriam (1994) War and Peace in the Early Elementary Classroom. *Children's Literature in Education.* Vol. 25, no. 2. (pp83-99)

Bercaw, Edna Coe. Illustrated by Robert Hunt (2000) *Halmoni's Day.* New York: Dial Books for Young Readers

Cai, Mingshui (2002) *Multicultural Literature for Children and Young Adults: Reflections on Critical Issues.* Westport: Greenwood Press

Choi, Sook Nyul (1993) *Echoes of the White Giraffe.* Boston: Houghton Mifflin Company

Choi, Sook Nyul (1991) *Year of Impossible Goodbyes*. New York: Bantam Doubleday Dell Books for Young Readers

Cumings, Bruce (1997) *Korea's Place in the Sun*. New York: W.W. Norton & Company

Cumings, Bruce (2004) *Origins of the Korean War*. Ithaca: Cornell University Press

Eckert, Carter; Lee, Ki-Baik; Lew, Young Ick; Robinson, Michael and Wagner, Edward W. (1991) *Korea Old and New: A History*. Cambridge: Harvard University Press

Galbraith, Mary (2000) What Must I Give Up In Order to Grow Up? The Great War and Childhood Survival Strategies in Transatlantic Picture Books. *The Lion and the Unicorn*. Vol. 24, no. 3. (pp337-359)

Goodman, Robin F. and Fahnestock, Andrea Henderson (2002) *The Day Our World Changed: Children's Art of 9/11*. New York: Harry N Abrams

Hade, Daniel D (1997) Reading Children's Literature Multiculturally. In Beckett, Sandra L. (Ed.) *Reflections of Change: Children's Literature Since 1945*. Westport: Greenwood Press, (pp115-122)

Harada, Violet (1998) Caught Between Two Worlds: Themes of Family, Community, and Ethnic Identity in Yoshiko Uchida's Works for Children. *Children's Literature in Education*. Vol. 29, no. 1. (pp19-30)

Henderson, Darwin L. and May, Jill P. (Eds.) (2005) *Exploring Culturally Diverse Literature for Children and Young Adults: Learning to Listen in New Ways*. Boston: Pearson Education, Inc.

Hollindale, Peter (1997) 'Children of Eyam': The Dramatisation of History. *Children's Literature in Education*. Vol. 28, no. 4. (pp205-218)

Kertzer, Adrienne (1999) "Do You Know What 'Auschwitz' Means?" Children's Literature and the Holocaust. *The Lion and the Unicorn*. Vol. 23, no. 2. (pp238-256)

Kidd, Kenneth. (2005) "A" is for Auschwitz: Psychoanalysis, Trauma Theory, and the "Children's Literature of Atrocity." *Children's Literature*. Vol.3 3 (pp120-148)

Larrick, Nancy (1965) The All-White World of Children's Literature. *Saturday Review*. September 11, 1965. (pp63-85)

Lowry, Lois (1999) *The Giver*. New York: Bantam Books for Young Readers

Myers, Mitzi (2000) Storying War: A Capsule Overview. *The Lion and the Unicorn*. Vol. 24, no. 3. (pp327-336)

Nodelman, Perry and Reimer, Mavis (2003) *The Pleasures of Children's Literature*. Boston: Allyn and Bacon

Oberdorfer, Don (1997) *The Two Koreas: a Contemporary History*. New York: Basic Books

Park, Frances and Park, Ginger (1998) *My Freedom Trip: a Child's Escape from North Korea*. Honesdale: Boyds Mills Press

Park, Linda Sue (2002) *When My Name was Keoko*. New York: Clarion Books

Park, Sarah (2005) School Stories: the Lore of Korean American Children in Picture Books. Paper presented at the annual meeting of the *Association for Asian American Studies*, Los Angeles, California

Rochman, Hazel (1993) *Against Borders: Promoting Books for a Multicultural World*. Chicago: American Library Association

Sims, Rudine (1982) *Shadow and Substance: Afro-American Experience in Contemporary Children's Fiction*. Urbana: National Council of Teachers of English

Sims Bishop, Rudine (Ed.) (1994) *Kaleidoscope: A Multicultural Booklist for Grades K-8*. Urbana: National Council of Teachers of English

Smith, Katherine Capshaw (2005) Forum: Trauma and Children's Literature. *Children's Literature*. Vol. 33 (pp115-119)

Sung, Kiwan and Min, Deok-gi (1996) Positive Images and Interesting Characters in Children's Literature. *Journal of Children's Literature* Vol. 22, no. 2 Spring. (pp9-11)

Takaki, Ronald (1998) *Strangers from a Different Shore: a History of Asian Americans*. Boston: Back Bay Books

Toelken, Barre (1996) *The Dynamics of Folklore*. Utah: Utah State University Press

Walter, Virginia A. (2000) Making Sense Out of Senselessness: The Social Construction of Adolescent Reality in the War Novels of Robert Westall. *The Lion and the Unicorn*. Vol. 24, no. 3. (pp432-444)

Yokota, Junko (1993) Literature about Asians and Asian Americans: Implications for Elementary Classrooms. In Miller, Suzanne M & McCaskill, Barbara (Eds.) *Multicultural Literature and Literacies: Making Space for Difference*. New York: State University of New York Press (pp229-246)

Yuh, Ji-Yeon (2002) *Beyond the Shadow of Camptown: Korean Military Brides in America*. New York: New York University Press

Websites

http://www.calstatela.edu/centers/ckaks/census/100_year_summary.ppt
Accessed on 12.27.06

http://www.census.gov/prod/2002pubs/c2kbr01-16.pdf
Accessed on 12.27.06

http://www.auschwitz-muzeum.oswiecim.pl/html/eng/muzeum/rada_muzeum.html
Accessed on 12.27.06

http://www.sarahpark.com
Accessed on 12.27.06

The New Hero: Franklin Delano Roosevelt, *The Prisoner of Zenda*, and a New Era of Adventure

Alison Pipitone

Franklin D. Roosevelt, 32nd President of the USA, was much influenced as a boy by the romances of Anthony Hope. By looking closely at the man who became President and cast such a long shadow over the American landscape, we catch glimpses of the young boy who grew up with adventure stories fuelling his imagination. Along with the books' somewhat trivial values came something deeper: the presence of an individual, stripped of traditional loyalties, who nonetheless possessed a strong moral compass.

Introduction

The link between the books of Anthony Hope and the leadership style of Franklin Delano Roosevelt is not an obvious one. Anthony Hope joined the ranks of popular British writers during the last decade of the nineteenth century, when adventure, leisure and a pursuit of the arts were very much in vogue. Along with the somewhat trivial values came something deeper: the presence of an individual, stripped of traditional loyalties, who nonetheless possessed a strong moral compass.

We know from comments by Franklin Roosevelt's mother and letters he wrote when he was a boy that Anthony Hope was among his favourite authors. The young FDR thrilled at the notion of adventure, a trait which he carried throughout his life. Ultimately, Roosevelt is viewed as an embodiment of western progress and democracy during the first half of the twentieth century. While totalitarian governments emerged after World War I, so too did the high-spirited idealism exemplified by Roosevelt. The following pages will explore the kind of hero depicted by Anthony Hope in *The Prisoner of Zenda*(Hope,1894)as it applies to the maturation and evolution of Franklin Delano Roosevelt.

Landscape of the new hero

'To meet Franklin Delano Roosevelt "with all his buoyant sparkle, his iridescence," Churchill once said, was like "opening a bottle of champagne."' (Meacham, 2003: xii) Roosevelt's enthusiasm, optimism, and effervescence were innate components of his nature, and became characteristics of his life and legacy. Franklin Roosevelt is widely considered the greatest U.S. president of the twentieth century, having navigated the United States through both the Great Depression and

World War II. His legacy is not without detractors, and his presidency was not without missteps and serious mistakes. These are well documented, and Roosevelt was, like all of us, a product of his time. In terms of historical significance, however, FDR's presence on the American and European landscape during the first half of the twentieth century cannot be underestimated. The celebrated historian and intellectual Isaiah Berlin wrote:

> The most insistent propaganda in those days declared that humanitarianism and liberalism and democratic forces were played out, and that the choice now lay between two bleak extremes, Communism and Fascism - the red or the black. To those who were not carried away by this patter the only light that was left in the darkness was the administration of Roosevelt and the New Deal in the United States. At a time of weakness and mounting despair in the democratic world Roosevelt radiated confidence and strength. He was the leader of the democratic world, and upon him alone, of all the statesmen in the '30s, no cloud rested - neither on him nor on the New Deal, which to European eyes still looks a bright chapter in the history of mankind.
> (Berlin, 1998: 25)

How Roosevelt came to represent these ideals to Berlin and to millions of people throughout the world and across the decades can be attributed to a variety of factors. FDR was a person who continually evolved during his 62 years of life. He was made kinder by the obstacles he overcame and made stronger by the tumultuous events of history he witnessed. One of the factors that played a role in Roosevelt's growth, and one that is largely under-represented in the hundreds of volumes written on his life and legacy, is the presence of books in his universe. In his personal collection Roosevelt owned over 15,000 books, including an assortment of naval histories, rare editions, popular fiction, scientific studies, and a large assortment of adventure.

FDR appreciated his vast collection from two perspectives; one, with an eye towards rare editions, and the other for the value contained within. In fact, one of the accomplishments of which Roosevelt was most proud was the establishment of the Franklin Delano Roosevelt Presidential Library and Museum, which created a national record that previously had not existed, and 'forever changed the way our nation cares for and preserves the papers of its presidents.' (Koch, 2005: 90) When he dedicated the library in 1941, the same year that America entered

World War II, Roosevelt said,

> It seems to me the dedication of a library is in itself an act of faith.
> To bring together the records of the past and to house them in
> buildings where they will be preserved for the use of men and
> women in the future, a nation must believe in three things. It must
> believe in the past. It must believe in the future. It must, above all,
> believe in the capacity of its own people so to learn from the past
> that they can gain in judgment in creating their own future. (Koch,
> 2005: 92)

Franklin Roosevelt possessed an insatiable curiosity and a boundless
enthusiasm towards the world. His reality was largely a creation of the
exterior, and his interior was quite unknown to even those who were
closest to him. Roosevelt used deception and ambiguity as a tool, both
politically and personally. Joe Persico writes, 'By the time FDR became
president, dissimulation had become second nature, and subterfuge
cloaked in geniality became his stock-in-trade.' (Persico, 2001: 6) We
will see in the following pages that this persona, the evasive, flippant,
yet convivial hero, is exactly the type of protagonist to whom FDR was
introduced in books such as *The Prisoner of Zenda*.

There are three specific periods of Franklin Roosevelt's life when
reading and books made an indelible mark upon his person. During
World War II, when both Roosevelt and Churchill needed vast reserves
of strength and stamina, literature played an important role in bolstering
their spirits. In speeches, radio addresses, and print, quotes by their
favourite authors underscored themes of courage and perseverance.
And during the most difficult times, poetry made its way across the
Atlantic in personal letters signed affectionately from "Winston" or
"Franklin." One example from January 1940 takes a passage from
Henry Wadsworth Longfellow's *The Building of a Ship*:

> Dear Churchill,
> I think this verse applies to your people as it does to us.
>   Sail on, O Ship of State!
>   Sail on, O Union, strong and great!
>   Humanity with all its fears,
>   With all the hopes of future years,
>   Is hanging breathless on thy fate!
> As ever yours,
> Franklin D. Roosevelt (Meacham, 2003: 95)

Twenty years prior to the war, Roosevelt had another use for literature.
In August 1921, at the age of 39, he was stricken with infantile

paralysis. For two years Roosevelt was almost completely bedridden, and this is a second period of time when reading was vital to his well-being.

> Then and later, there was much speculation about the effects of Roosevelt's struggle against infantile paralysis on his personality and character...But some people who knew him believed that the inner man had undergone a transformation. Polio, they said, had strengthened his character, purged him of the vestiges of superficiality and arrogance, and most important, imbued him with a deep sympathy for the disadvantaged. (Maney, 1992: 27)

Eleanor Roosevelt remarked that this struggle turned her husband into a deeper, more thoughtful, and kinder human being. We know from letters and recollections that FDR found solace in writing letters, poring over his stamp collection, and doing a vast amount of reading during these years.

Third, and what will be the focus of the following pages, is the presence and importance of literature in Roosevelt's life as a young boy. In his article *The Literary Education of Franklin Delano Roosevelt*, Cyril Clemens writes

> The lack of friends and relatives his own age encouraged Roosevelt's interest in reading. His knowledge of the world was enhanced through the devouring of the large book collection at the Hyde Park mansion, Springwood. (Bestor, 1955)

Specifically, I will look at Anthony Hope's *The Prisoner of Zenda* as a typical example of Roosevelt's favourite kind of book - the adventure story. According to Roosevelt's mother, Anthony Hope was FDR's 'favourite'.

In fact, Anthony Hope was one of several Roosevelt favourites, a group which also included Rudyard Kipling and Mark Twain. In 1897, when he was 15 years old and studying at Groton, Roosevelt included the following in a letter to his parents: 'I am reading '*Phroso*,' the new book by Anthony Hope. It is awfully exciting and I cannot leave it for one moment.' (Roosevelt, Elliot, 1947:88) *Phroso* (Hope), the follow-up to *The Prisoner of Zenda*, did not achieve the same level of success as its predecessor; however, it included similar themes of adventure and a similar version of heroism. From Roosevelt's statements to his parents, we get a sense of the exuberance with which he experienced the adventure story.

The Prisoner of Zenda

The climate in which Anthony Hope's *The Prisoner of Zenda* was received is an important area of consideration. In the United States in the 1890's, one-eighth of the population controlled seven-eighths of the income. (*World Book Multimedia Encyclopedia*: 2003) Industrialization and immigration created a huge working class, underpaid and unprotected by a government that was just beginning to grapple with labour law. Franklin's father, James Roosevelt, who was the vice-president of the Delaware and Hudson Railway, and who counted the Vanderbilts and the Astors as his neighbours, was among the wealthiest Americans. For this stratum of American society, protecting their wealth was a necessity and helping the poor was at best, a slight concern. The rumblings of a beleaguered working class were kept at a comfortable distance.

It is upon this cultural landscape that the United States saw a medieval revivalism which idealized a simplified, clear social structure. According to Karen Roggenkamp, 'fiction was only part of a widespread medievalist movement...evident as well in architecture, visual arts, philosophy, and virtually every other sector of American culture.' (Roggenkamp, 2000: 37) Part of the appeal included romantic and unfamiliar settings, which in the case of *The Prisoner of Zenda* is the fictional eastern European country Ruritania.

A brief synopsis of *The Prisoner of Zenda* finds Rudolf Rassendyll, a well-to-do but somewhat unambitious young man, about to take on a mundane yet acceptable position as a diplomat's assistant. Rudolf Rassendyll is distantly related to the royal family of Ruritania and has the trademark 'Elphberg red' hair and long nose. (Hope, 1894: 23) He decides to attend the coronation of the new King, Rudolf Elphberg. He cannot tell anyone in his family where he is going, because it would be improper for him to travel to that country, and hence we have the setup for an adventure. From the very beginning we are aware of the fact that Rudolf is a bit unconcerned with protocol. Note the following conversation with his very proper sister-in-law:

> "The difference between you and Robert," said my sister-in-law..."is that he recognises the duties of his position, and you only see the opportunities of yours."
> "To a man of spirit, My dear Rose," I answered, "opportunities are duties." (Hope, 1894: 11)

Throughout the story, Rassendyll stands as an observer of his own class, and maintains a benevolent curiosity towards both the royalty and the peasants he encounters in Ruritania. As an impartial narrator, Rudolf Rassendyll is able to expose discrepancies and ironies through use of simple exposition.

It is soon discovered that Rudolph Rassendyll looks almost exactly like the king. Through a series of events and after an assassination attempt, Rassendyll must play the part of the king for the coronation and beyond. 'King Rudolf is a hard-drinking, feckless playboy, unpopular with the common people, but supported by the aristocracy, the Church, the army, and the wealthier classes in general.' (*Publishers Weekly*,1933) When Rudolf Rassendyll impersonates the king, he starts to repair the king's reputation. He rides without his helmet and without the protection of guards through the city streets, claiming, "'I will have my people see that their King trusts them.'" (Hope, 1894: 42) The people respond with cheers and allegiance.

In the midst of all this is the presence of Princess Flavia, betrothed to the king, who falls in love with Rassendyll. Ultimately, Rassendyll and the princess profess their love for one another but realize they cannot stay together. The crown is safely restored to Rudolf Elphberg, who has acquired some measure of humility and concern for the people of Ruritania after his ordeal.

An important concept for consideration is the presence of Princess Flavia as a heroine who does not shirk her sense of duty for love. This idea was quite progressive in 1894, when a predominantly Victorian view of women saw them as delicate and intellectually limited creatures. In direct contrast to this precept, Princess Flavia does not hesitate to choose her kingdom over her lover. In a melodramatic scene where the two decide their fate, an essential theme emerges which places the princess on equal ground with her male counterpart. Flavia says,

> "If love were the only thing, I would follow you - in rags, if need be - to the world's end; for you hold my heart in the hollow of your hand! But is love the only thing?... Honour binds a woman too, Rudolf. My honour lies in being true to my country and my House. I don't know why God has let me love you; but I know I must stay." (Hope, 1894: 179)

Rudolf Rassendyll returns home, tells no one about his adventure, and resumes his life. However, he is changed, and he writes:

> Since all these events whose history I have set down happened I have lived a very quiet life... The ordinary ambitions and aims of men in my position seem to me dull and unattractive. I have little fancy for the whirl of society, and none for the jostle of politics. Lady Burlesdon utterly despairs of me; my neighbours think me an indolent, dreamy unsociable fellow... Sometimes I have a notion...that my part in life is not altogether played; that, somehow and some day, I shall mix again in great affairs, I shall again spin policies in a busy brain, match my wits against my enemies', brace my muscles to fight a good fight and strike stout blows. (Hope, 1894: 188)

When *The Prisoner of Zenda* was published in London in January 1894, it was wildly popular. The following is from Hope's 'faithfully-kept diary' on November 22nd of that year (Randall, 1939: 4): 'Zenda still moves - about 12,000 have been sold - and moves still more in America.' The book was:

> ...an instantaneous success, appearing on the best seller lists for the next twenty years...[Hope's] novels, introducing something distinctly different in popular literature, in the creation of an imaginary kingdom somewhere in the Balkans, were the craze of a generation, and he had many imitators. (*Publishers Weekly*, 1933)

With Zenda, Hope ushered in a character that is initially unremarkable, but rises to heroic stature after a series of challenges. A significant aspect is that the new hero operates *within* the establishment rather than proposing an alternative to it. While he doesn't seek to change the essence of his environment, he learns to rebel in subtle ways. The new hero also expresses a concern for those less fortunate than himself, and views women as equals rather than creatures in need of guidance and protection. This hero does not idealize or idolize the wealthy, the well born, the well connected; in other words, those who hold the power. Perhaps most importantly, the acts of heroism or iniquity are based on a personal code rather than a sweeping more conventional standard. This new hero ascribes to his - and in some cases, her - own conscience, driven by personal rather than societal impetus. It signifies the emergence of the individual over the collective, which is a trend that continued throughout the twentieth century in the West.

When the young Franklin Roosevelt read *The Prisoner of Zenda* and other books of this genre, he was presented with examples of self-determination and loyalty to one's own particular principles. A code of conduct, although initiated by upbringing, education, and access to opportunity, was reinforced through the adventures recounted in books such as *The Prisoner of Zenda*.

Echoes of the new hero

According to Franklin Roosevelt's mother,

> We never chose books for Franklin. We preferred that he make his own selection from the houseful we had accumulated over a period of years. But if we had tried to supervise his selection, we could not have come upon a more wholesome array than he chose for himself. (Mrs. James Roosevelt, 1933: 14)

Franklin Roosevelt enjoyed books that were popular, exciting and typical of a young man experiencing the world at the turn of the twentieth century. The adventure story, with its attending messages about the nature of power resonated with FDR's own personality and surroundings. FDR encountered themes of subtle heroism, irreverence towards authority, and a concept of leadership tempered by humour in *The Prisoner of Zenda*, all of which reinforced qualities already part of his own makeup.

Another message offered by Zenda is the presence a strong woman, one who is consistently regarded as an equal to the male protagonist. Similarly, the young FDR met a young woman to whom he was attracted for reasons more than simply physical:

> At a Christmas party in 1898...a sixteen-year old Franklin, then a Groton student, had asked an unhappy, pathetically dressed fourteen-year old Eleanor to dance, for which she had been deeply grateful.... It was about this time, too, that he was said to have remarked to his mother, "Cousin Eleanor has a very good mind." (Lash, 1971: 150)

The subsequent relationship between Franklin and Eleanor Roosevelt was complicated; however, their respect for one another was never in question.

The allure of adventure enticed Franklin Roosevelt throughout his life. For example, while he was a student at Harvard, he:

> devised a code, numerals substituting for vowels, and symbols...substituting for consonants, all running together giving no hint of where words started or ended. Though child's play for a

serious cryptanalyst, the code nevertheless served Franklin's need
for and pleasure in secrecy. (Persico, 2001: 5)

At the time, Roosevelt used this code in a sort of diary, professing his
love for a young lady at school. Years later, the passion with which
Roosevelt undertook a task of deception was similar, but the stakes
were much higher.

Popular consensus in the United States was largely isolationist in 1940,
despite the fact that much of Europe had already fallen to Hitler and the
Nazis. Doris Kearns Goodwin writes,

> ...the isolationists insisted that the United States was protected from
> harm by its oceans and could best lead by sustaining democracy at
> home. Responding to the overwhelming strength of isolationist
> sentiment in the country at large, the Congress had passed a series
> of Neutrality Acts in the mid-1930's...Roosevelt had tried on
> occasion to shift the prevailing opinion...but when the press evinced
> shock at what they termed a radical shift in foreign policy and
> isolationist congressmen threatened impeachment, Roosevelt had
> pulled back. "It's a terrible thing," he told his aide Sam Rosenman,
> "to look over your shoulder when you are trying to lead - and find no
> one there." He had resolved at that point to move one step at a
> time, to nurse the country along to a more sophisticated view of the
> world, to keep from getting too far ahead of the electorate.
> (Goodwin, 1994: 22-23)

Both Roosevelt and Churchill recognized the desperate need for an
American presence in the war in order to prevent Hitler from taking
England. But by placating Churchill, Roosevelt would risk his political
future, and greater consequences if Britain indeed fell. The two leaders
understood the fundamental importance of an alliance, but they did not
know how to proceed. So in true adventure story fashion, they agreed
upon a secret meeting off the coast of Newfoundland in order to forge a
plan. The President proceeded to lie to the media, his cabinet, most of
his advisors, and even his wife in order to pull off the meeting. John
Meacham writes about this episode:

> "I was faced with a practical problem of extreme difficulty,"
> Roosevelt later wrote in a private memorandum. He wanted to effect
> a clandestine session with Churchill off Newfoundland in August
> 1941 to, as Roosevelt put it, "talk over the problem of the defeat of
> Germany.... The utmost secrecy before and during the trip was
> essential," Roosevelt recalled. "This was, of course, obvious
> because the Prime Minister would traverse, both going and
> returning from Newfoundland, long distances in dangerous

waters"... Roosevelt also wanted to keep his critics quiet until the meeting was over. The United States was still neutral, and after Lend-Lease, the last thing he needed was to hand the isolationists something else to use against him.

Roosevelt took matters into his own hands, telling reporters he might take a cruise on the *USS Potomac* in Maine "to get some cool nights" that summer. "This," Roosevelt recalled with a touch of boys' adventure novel prose, "became the basis for the plan of escape." (Meacham, 2003: 102)

> The President went so far as to invent the name of one of the places he might visit on this trip. Several reporters spent days trying to pinpoint where exactly The Cherable Isles - a Roosevelt invention - were located. (Bestor, 1955: 91)

Jon Meacham describes the President's excitement for the escapade:

> Let the proud author of the plot explain what happened next: "Strange thing happened this morning - suddenly found ourselves transferred with all our baggage & mess crew from the little *Potomac* to the Great Big Cruiser *Augusta!*... And then, the Island of Martha's Vineyard disappeared in the distance, and as we head out into the Atlantic all we can see of our protecting escort, a heavy cruiser and four destroyers. Curiously enough the Potomac still flies my flag & tonight will be seen by thousands as she passes quietly through the Cape Cod Canal, guarded on shore by Secret Service and State Troopers while in fact the Pres. will be about 250 miles away." (Meacham, 2003: 105)

The exuberance with which FDR approached this deception is palpable. Ultimately, the meeting between Roosevelt and Churchill was successful. The trip cemented a friendship between the two leaders, and set in motion an alliance of monumental proportions.

Conclusion

It is my belief that the person we are as a child is essentially the adult we become. One's inherent nature is not fundamentally changed, regardless of circumstance, fortune, and choices made along the way. What a child chooses to read on his or her own volition reflects resounding themes, and offers an important contribution to his or her development. By looking closely at the man who became President and cast such a long shadow over the American landscape, we catch glimpses of the young boy who grew up with adventure stories fuelling his imagination.

In *No Ordinary Time*, Doris Kearns Goodwin recounts a poignant example of FDR's attachment to childhood:

> On nights filled with tension and concern, Franklin Roosevelt performed a ritual that helped him fall asleep. He would close his eyes and imagine himself at Hyde Park as a boy, standing with his sled in the snow atop the steep hill that stretched far below. As he accelerated down the hill, he manoeuvred each familiar curve with perfect skill until he reached the bottom, whereupon, pulling his sled behind him, he started slowly back up until he reached the top, where he would once more begin his descent. Again and again he replayed this remembered scene in his mind, obliterating his awareness of the shrunken legs inert beneath the sheets, undoing the knowledge that he would never climb a hill or even walk on his own power again. Thus liberating himself from his paralysis through an act of imaginative will, the president of the United States would fall asleep. (Goodwin, 1994)

Perhaps too in those quiet moments of imagination there were appearances by fortune-hunters and rogues, ladies and lords. Perhaps Rudolf Rassendyll and Princess Flavia were reunited by a gentle hand of fate. Maybe on those nights the White House grounds, like the forests of Ruritania, were filled with sounds of mystery and danger, and shouts of courage and of hope. Perhaps the adventure continued long after the book was closed.

Bibliography

Berlin, Isaiah (1998) *Personal Impressions*. Princeton, New Jersey: Princeton University Press

Bestor, Arthur, Mearns, David C. Jonathan Daniels (1955) *Three Presidents and Their Books*. Urbana: University of Illinois Press

Fogel, Nancy (ed.) (2005) *FDR at Home*. Poughkeepsie: Dutchess County Historical Society

Geddes, Donald Porter (ed.) (1945) *Franklin Delano Roosevelt: A Memorial*. New York: Pocket Books, Inc.

Goodwin, Doris Kearns (1994) *No Ordinary Time: Franklin and Eleanor Roosevelt: The Home Front in World War II*. New York: Simon & Schuster

Grafton, John (ed.) (1999) *Franklin Delano Roosevelt: Great Speeches*. Mineola, New York: Dover Publications, Inc.

Hope, Anthony (1894) *The Prisoner of Zenda.* London: J.M. Dent & Sons Ltd

How Hope Worked (1911) *The Bookman.* (pp451-453)

Kinnaird, Clark (1945) *The Real F.D.R.* New York: The Citadel Press

Koch, Cynthia M. & Bassanese, Lynn A. (2005) Roosevelt and His Library. In Fogel, Nancy (ed.) *FDR at Home.* Poughkeepsie: Dutchess County Historical Society, (pp90-106)

Maney, Patrick J (1992) *The Roosevelt Presence: A Biography of Franklin Delano Roosevelt.* New York: Twayne Publishers

Meacham, John (2003) *Franklin and Winston: An Intimate Portrait of an Epic Friendship.* New York: Random House

Obituary: Anthony Hope. (1933) *The Publishers Weekly.* Vol. 124 (p23)

Persico, Joseph E. (2001) *Roosevelt's Secret War: FDR and WWII Espionage.* New York: Random House

Randall, D.A. (1939) One Hundred Good Novels; The Prisoner of Zenda. *The Publishers Weekly.* Volume 136 (pp541-543)

Roggenkamp, Karen. (2000) The Evangelina Cisneros Romance, Medievalist Fiction, and the Journalism that Acts. *Journal of American and Comparative Cultures.* Volume 23 (pp25-37)

Roosevelt, Elliott (ed.) (1970) *F.D.R. His Personal Letters: Early Years.* New York: Duell, Sloan, and Pearce

Roosevelt, Mrs. James, as told to Isabel Leighton, Gabrielle Forbush (1933) *My Boy Franklin.* New York: Ray Long & Richard R. Smith, Inc.

Unknown (2003) History of the United States: Gay Nineties. *World Book Multimedia Encyclopedia*, 2003 Edition. Version 7.1.1

Activating the Shadow: Dark Fiction for Children

Jennifer Sattaur

Jung's Archetype of the Shadow can throw a new light on the ways in which we react to disturbing literature. An analysis of various works of contemporary children's fiction demonstrates how the traditional barrier between child and adult may be beneficially broken down, ways in which disturbing literature can be beneficial, and how effective the books are in activating a psychical response in the reader. The most valuable way in which a text can present disturbing Shadow elements is one in which those elements are left unresolved, so that the reader is given an opportunity to internalise the conflicts and tensions and work through them; far from damaging the children they are allowed to work upon, the texts may actually be beneficial in furthering the process of individuation, by allowing an engagement with the Shadow Archetype.

The child lives in a pre-rational and above all in a pre-scientific world, the world of the men who existed before us. Our roots lie in that world and every child grows from those roots. (Jung, 1991: 144)

This account of the child is a fitting introduction to the ways in which I wish to use a Jungian analysis of various works of contemporary children's fiction to demonstrate how the traditional barrier between child and adult may be beneficially broken down, and how analytical psychology thereby holds the potential to throw a new light on the ways in which we react to disturbing literature. Starting with a discussion of Jungian analysis applied to children's literature and the ways in which we segregate childhood from adulthood, I move on to an examination of the Archetype of the Shadow, and the ways in which disturbing literature can be beneficial. Finally, I examine five works of contemporary children's fiction for the patterns of Shadow Archetype they present, and their effectiveness in activating a psychical response in the reader.

Protection v. horror: the case

Despite the huge potential within analytical psychology for engagement with children's literature, I believe that the majority of readings in this area have been weak in comparison to other critical approaches. Nicholas Tucker, for example, gives the following summary, which offers an insight into how many critics approach Jungian analysis:

> For Carl Jung, fairy tales are often symbolic of the individual's struggle from the primitive, animal level to the world of higher consciousness and personal fulfilment. Forests, monsters, castles, valued helpers and all the various trials encountered on the way are aspects of the positive and negative side of the reader's own self.(Tucker, 1992: 164-5)

I feel that this is overly simplified, and that it offers a reductive method of applying the rich material presented by analytical psychology. Analysis of children's literature often attempts to view the text as a psychological crutch, while analysis of fairy tales, on the other hand, has concentrated more on the adult readership. I would argue, however, that within Analytical Psychology there is the potential for breaking down the barrier usually constructed between child and adult, and that without that barrier stronger readings of 'children's' literature are possible.

Within children's literature, the weakest readings are those which are reductive, forcing the symbols that emerge within a text into a rigid psychological pattern by assigning characters an Archetypal function, and events a place in the individuation process, limiting the text to only one interpretation. Should that interpretation fail to be relevant to the reader, it loses its impact. However, throughout his writings, Jung attempts to make clear the distinction between *Archetype* and *Archetypal image*. In *The Phenomenology of Spirit in Fairytales*, Jung describes the 'interplay of the Archetypes'. This phrase suggests what Jung was anxious to make clear: that no single Archetypal image can be pinned down and accurately identified in correspondence to a particular Archetype. To assign image to Archetype within a text is a risky business; the image may have any number of interpretations and may belong to any Archetype, depending upon the individual interpreter:

> There are a number of Jungian interpretations of children's novels that identify various characters as the protagonist's shadow or anima, and describe how the story replicates an individual's move towards psychic integration... If they do, though, why would a reader who has gone through the process once and become an integrated whole as a result of it ever again read or want to read a similar book that replicated the experience? (Nodelman, 2000: 6)

Nodelman's question is relevant; this is not the way Jungian criticism should be working.

Rather, for each reader a single image may correspond to many different Archetypes, or to an 'interplay' between many. The critic's task is to use Jungian analysis to identify *patterns* of images within a text that are strong enough to activate a particular psychical response in the reader. Such a reading does not assign an individual interpretation to an image, but rather picks up on patterns of images and attempts to link them back to an Archetypal pattern, speculating on the psychical response a reader might have. This brings us to the question of reader response, particularly where disturbing material is concerned.

There are certain ways of presenting disturbing elements which seek to resolve the issues they present, and certain ways of presenting them which leave them unresolved and problematical. The question is, which method of presentation is preferable? Marie-Louise von Franz states that:

> When you tell fairy tales to children, they at once and naively identify and get all the feeling of the story... it gives a model for living, an encouraging vivifying model which reminds one unconsciously of all life's positive possibilities. (Franz, 1996: 63)

This, of course, depends entirely on the way in which the story is presented; if the tale fails to address the problems relevant to the reader, or if it resolves them too completely, the model may be flat and uninspiring rather than 'vivifying'. I would argue that, in contrast, a refusal to protect the child from the full impact of disturbing material allows archetypal patterns to emerge more freely and gives them more chance of having an effect.

As controversies over works such as the *Harry Potter* series have shown, the concern over whether certain works are appropriate for children or not is one that has by no means diminished in the twentieth and twenty-first centuries. For example, Bettelheim wrote in 1977 that: 'To depreciate protective imagery... is to rob the young child of one aspect of the prolonged safety and comfort he needs...' (1977: 50), and although Bettelheim concedes that one of the benefits of the Fairy Tale is that it teaches the child to cope with difficult and traumatic life situations, he also feels that it is necessary to resolve these situations for the child through the medium of a happy ending. Nicholas Tucker agrees: 'Moments of fear have their place in stories for the young, however, so long as they are successfully contained by a plot that ends on a reassuring, consoling note' (1981: 62). I believe that the view that disturbing elements should be resolved, although widespread, is questionable; the matter is not as straightforward as Bettelheim would have us believe. The child inherently knows that life is harsh, dark and frightening - at least according to child psychologists such as Fordham and Winnicott. What concerns the child is not that fear and evil exist, but what to *do* about them. It is therefore possible that to protect the child deprives him not of much needed security, but rather of the motivation for further development. According to Jung, the Shadow - a vague term which more or less equates to the dark side of human nature - is the first Archetype which must be encountered and assimilated in order for the process of individuation to kick-off. Therefore, literature which challenges a child to grapple with the Shadow is more likely to help him develop a healthy relationship with Shadow elements early in life. In Analytical Psychology the development of Self is a lifelong process which moves smoothly from the child's development of consciousness to the adult's perfection of the unified mind, as a result of the assimilation, throughout life, of unconscious elements. I would argue that there is no reason to draw a line at puberty dividing this process in half. Rather, the process of growing up is one that lasts a life-time, and the introduction of the child to grown-up things can challenge him to work harder at assimilating and coming to terms with them. A surprising piece of psychological evidence from the 1920s supports this theory; Christopher Fortune describes how Sandov and Ferenczi, in 1923, discovered that: '...traumatised young children often had accelerated developmental characteristics, including highly acute sensitivities and intuitions - in short, wisdom beyond their years' (2003: 457). Sandov and Ferenczi were most likely concerned with serious traumatic events in a child's life; however, it seems to me possible that second-hand trauma - received through disturbing literature - might have a similar effect on childhood development. (This is, of course, kinder - not to mention morally and legally more acceptable - than exposing young children to first-hand trauma.) In other words, stress can become a positive factor in the process of individuation.

There is, therefore, every reason to suppose that literature which is disturbing without resolving essential problems for the reader will have a beneficial effect on psychic development. It is important that we learn to trust children to enter into such dialogues as much as we trust adults to do so. As Piaget, among others, demonstrated, the inherent wisdom of the child is equal to that of the adult; it simply requires activation (Ginsberg & Cooper, 1979). The child may not be able to understand everything that the adult can, but he *can* cope with the process of understanding.

Releasing the shadow

In this final section of the paper, I will attempt to assess the ways in which Jungian analysis of literature can reveal patterns of the Shadow Archetype which might (and only *might*) assist in activating the psychic processes of the reader. By patterns, I mean to show that themes, rather than specific characters or events, which appear in the text indicate that the Shadow Archetype might be at work. I hope that the concentration on multiple images rather than specific ones will in part free the analysis from the straight jacketing Jungian analyses sometimes fall prey to. The Shadow Archetype, in this context, would refer to those elements of a story which indicate the dark side of human nature which must be accepted along with the good. Tom Baker's *The Boy Who Kicked Pigs* (1999), Robert Westall's *Blitzcat* (1989), Philip Pullman's *His Dark Materials* (1995, 1997, 2000), Lemony Snicket's *A Series of Unfortunate Events* (2001), and Eoin Colfer's *Artemis Fowl* (2001), are all examined for indications of Shadow patterns, and the responses those patterns might evoke in readers. I would like to argue that while all five seek to present their readers with unsettling images and concepts, the first three have the potential to activate an engagement with the Shadow, while the last two keep it firmly under control.

The answer to the question of what exactly *is* a disturbing element, I feel, goes beyond foul language and violence. It also includes any elements which unsettle the notion of the self as good and the world as safe, the notion that things will work out in the end, the notion that evil can be eradicated. In different ways, all five of our texts contain such elements. In *The Boy Who Kicked Pigs* the protagonist, after causing a highway explosion in which hundreds die, accidentally becomes trapped in his tree hideaway, where he is gnawed to death by rats. *Blitzcat* is the story of a cat during World War I attempting to find her master; through the course of the book the cat experiences one of her kittens being killed by a rat, risks being eaten in France and shot at in London, and comes close to being blown up by a stray bomb, which ruins her hearing and blasts the two humans next to her into smithereens. The combination of the cruelty of war-torn human beings and the cat's un-human way of experiencing the world can be highly disturbing. *His Dark Materials* is perhaps the best known of my examples. Pullman's trilogy destroys the idea of a comfortable world and a safe afterlife:

> ... Pullman achieves a powerful and coherent narrative precisely by jettisoning popular notions of the soul living on in a happy afterlife

and by returning to older fears of the horror and finality of death...(Gooderham, 2003: 161-164)

The world view he presents is one where happiness must go hand in hand with suffering, and the only salvation is to live life to the fullest. Throughout his narrative, epic morality battles with a prevailing view that the end justifies the means. Even if it were not for the numerous deaths, betrayals, and other such violences, this world view would be enough to mark the novels as disturbing (Pullman, 1995, 1997, 2000).

Artemis Fowl and *A Series of Unfortunate Events* both contain elements which are unsettling. Artemis's position as a child master criminal, his uneasy relationship with his parents, and the violent means he uses to increase his family's fortune, are all potentially disturbing (Colfer, 2001, 2002, 2003). Lemony Snicket's novels are marketed on the appeal of their gloomy and disturbing plots, in which a trio of orphans watch their family and friends being killed off one by one, and experience the greed, cruelty, cowardice, and neglect of the people who should care for them. As Bruce Butt describes it: 'Snicket's world queasily combines a melodramatic escapism with the sinister menace of an all-too-real adult world.' (2003: 283) As I shall discuss below, however, the effect of the disturbing elements in these last two series are negated and thus are less effective at activating the psyche than those of the first three works.

The most important factor in determining whether the Shadow can emerge or not is, in my opinion, ambiguity. If a shadow element is present, but is then tidied away neatly, there is little opportunity for the reader to engage creatively and actively with it. In other words, a story that answers all the difficult questions leaves no space for a dialogue between the reader's psyche and the text. In this sense, both *Blitzcat* and *The Boy Who Kicked Pigs* are excellent at forcing the reader to find a way of coping with Shadow elements. In *The Boy Who Kicked Pigs*, there is no explanation or justification given for the evil in Robert Caligari's soul. His hatred and vindictiveness, for all the humour that Baker presents them with, are the dark and vicious instincts that every angry child is familiar with:

> This slaughter of the innocent [man-eating shark] confirmed to Robert how awful people can be. And he hated them. He decided to throw in his lot with otters, sharks and stoats, with poisonous snakes and with rats, with cockroaches and spiders... He would love the hated and hate the people... (Baker, 1999: 41)

His irrational hatreds are not, however, explained away or resolved, nor is the ridiculousness of Robert's victims. (It is worth noting that his hatred is first sparked off by the fact that people laugh at him for his obsessive need to kick pigs and pig-products). Although Robert dies and the Shadow elements are contained by his death, this does not completely or tidily solve the problem of his behaviour for the reader.

Similarly, in *Blitzcat*, the trick of telling the story from the cat's point of view has the effect of humanising the un-human actions and feelings of the cat, and of dehumanising the human behaviour of the shell-shocked people it encounters. Virginia A. Walter, in talking about Robert Westall's war novels as a collection, says:

> Westall leaves a lot of space for young readers to insert themselves
> in the text...making his novels rich fields of vicarious experiences,
> with a wealth of data to be incorporated into the child's own social
> reality. (Walter, 2000: 444)

Although the cat does experience a happy ending, the problem of inhuman or 'animalistic' behaviour contrasted to what ought to be human(e) values is left open for the reader to ponder in himself as well as in the story.

His Dark Materials is also ambiguous, despite its potentially happy ending. The novels are highly ideological and do not disguise their message; in that sense there is less ambiguity than would be desirable for the manifestations of the Shadow we are examining. For example, although the idea that Will and Lyra must separate forever, despite their love, is highly painful, Pullman resolves it by making it clear that they have made the right choice and that their suffering will be for the greater good. On the other hand, no solution is presented to counter the bleak picture of a universe without purpose and control, in which humans must find whatever meaning they can in themselves, without an outside referent: 'The subject of *His Dark Materials* is nothing less than the story of how human beings, at this critical time in history, might evolve toward a higher level of consciousness.' (Lenz, 2001: 123) Pullman does not portray this evolution as easy.

A Series of Unfortunate Events and *Artemis Fowl* while utilizing seemingly dark Shadow elements, are both lacking in this ambiguity. In the first, Snicket's overwhelming bleak humour softens the effect of the horrific in the lives of the orphans. Furthermore, the reader is left in no doubt about who the 'good guys' and the 'bad guys' are. John Walsh says:

> They teach the blunt lesson that good will not triumph over evil simply by being good, only by being lucky, being cunning or possessing superior fire-power. It's an unsettling, amoral and slightly melancholy lesson... (Walsh, 2002)

I would argue, however, that the black and white divisions between good and evil mean that, as unsettling as the lesson may be, it nevertheless does not create an ambiguous pattern of the Shadow. The good are always good, and the bad are always bad; the Baudelaires never put a toe out of line, and there is never a moment's mercy from Count Olaf. Similarly, Artemis's bad behaviour is always negated by the end of the story, showing him to have pity for those he exploits, and a working sense of right and wrong. As the series progresses, his repentance does too. This is in contrast to, for example, *Blitzcat*'s refusal to give the cat a human sense of moral value, and to Robert Calligari's lack of genuine repentance at his death.

Like a lack of ambiguity, an ending which resolves all Shadow elements in a text leaves the reader without much space in which to work through such elements for himself. The *Artemis Fowl* books tend to end on a positive note, excusing Artemis for his misdeeds, and ensuring that no ill consequences result. For example, in the epilogue to the first book we are told:

> There is a tendency to romanticise Artemis. To attribute to him qualities that he does not possess. The fact that he wished to heal his mother is not a sign of affection... He kept the existence of the People [fairies] quiet only so that he could continue to exploit them... (Colfer, 2002: 279)

However, as the epilogue states, there *is* a tendency to romanticise Artemis, and that is because his creator has made him a sympathetic character. The reader knows better than to believe the cynicism of the narrator of the epilogue, or of Artemis himself. We know that he loves his parents, and has both respect and pity for the People, and later books prove us right. In *A Series of Unfortunate Events* the orphans are still alive and hopeful, and the author's own gloomy predictions are softened by the humour which leaves no room for any real worry. Both of these series, then, are unlikely to stimulate an active engagement with the Shadow in the reader.

By contrast, the ambiguities of the three books in *His Dark Materials* find their climax in the bleak but hopeful ending to the trilogy. The endings to *Blitzcat* and *The Boy Who Kicked Pigs* are similarly ambiguous. The ending to *Blitzcat* is happy, in some senses. The cat finds her human at long last and, because he has been injured and invalided out of flying, there is no danger that he will disappear again. The book ends with a vision of the two of them happy together, almost like lovers reunited:

> Lord Gort wriggled over on her back, careful not to fall off his knee. Idly, she swung a paw in the direction of his tie. In her small mind, all the places, all the people were fading... Her great days were over, her story was finished... She was home with her person; she was warm, dry, full. That was all that mattered. (Westall, 2002: 228)

However, not only is the ambiguity mentioned earlier not resolved, but it is actually strengthened in the ending; the cat's owner is fully prepared to allow the airfield authorities to shoot her. It is only by luck that the cat does *not* reveal herself to those authorities, and the cat knows nothing of her owner's near betrayal of her devotion; a betrayal the cat would in all probability herself have committed had the positions been reversed. The reader is left to puzzle out the (in)humanity of this for himself.

The Boy Who Kicked Pigs ends on a note so grim it is the antithesis of a happy ending; the horror of Robert Caligari's death almost resolves the Shadow in the way a happy ending would have. The description is painful, as just a fragment will demonstrate:

> But there was to be no mercy or comfort for the boy who had never shown mercy to his victims in the days when he was strong and when his cunning had made him the master of innocent creatures. His pain and terror were now so great that Robert could imagine nothing worse. As this thought came to him the rat stopped chewing at Robert's nose. (Baker, 1999: 119-21)

There is not really any repentance in Robert, only horror at the irony and terror of his death. Luckily, Baker's humour encourages the reader to identify with Robert, saving the tale from being simply a grotesquely didactic cautionary tale along the lines of *Shockheaded Peter*. This, together with the ambiguities already mentioned above, leaves room for the reader to question the text and try and resolve the problem of Robert's 'evil' for himself. Thus, an engagement with the Shadow is probable.

To conclude, then, the most valuable way in which a text can present disturbing Shadow elements is one in which those elements are left unresolved, so that the reader is given an opportunity to internalise the conflicts and tensions and work through them for himself. A Jungian reading which, by analysing a text for the pattern which relates to certain archetypes, rather than simply labelling a single symbol in the text with an archetypal tag, can help to demonstrate this point, and others, effectively. Texts which do leave elements unresolved, far from damaging the children they are allowed to work upon, may actually be beneficial in furthering the process of individuation, by allowing an engagement with the Shadow Archetype.

Bibliography

Allain-Dupré, Brigitte (2005) What Does the Child Analyst Bring to Jungian Thought? *Journal of Analytical Psychology* Vol. 50, no. 3. (pp351-65)

Baker, Tom (1999) *The Boy Who Kicked Pigs.* London: Faber and Faber Ltd.

Barchers, Suzanne (1988) Beyond Disney: Reading and Writing Traditional and Alternative Fairy Tales. *Lion and the Unicorn* Vol. 12, no. 2. (pp135-50)

Bettelheim, Bruno (1977) *The Uses of Enchantment.* New York: Vintage Books, Random House

Butt, Bruce (2003) 'He's Behind You!': Reflections on Repetition and Predictability in Lemony Snicket's A Series of Unfortunate Events. *Children's Literature in Education* Vol. 34, no. 4. (pp277-86)

Colfer, Eoin (2001) *Artemis Fowl.* London: Viking

Colfer, Eoin (2002) *Artemis Fowl: The Arctic Incident.* London: Viking

Colfer, Eoin (2003) *Artemis Fowl: The Eternity Code.* London: Viking

Crago, Hugh (2003) What is a Fairy Tale? *Signal* Vol. 100. (pp8-26)

Echlin, Helen (2002) 'Dark Star', *The Guardian* 21 Aug, on-line: www.guardian.co.uk.

Fordham, M. (1994) *Children as Individuals.* 3rd ed. London: Free Association Books

Fortune, Christopher (2003) The Analytical Nursery: Ferenczi's 'Wise Baby' Meets Jung's 'Divine Child'. *Journal of Analytical Psychology* Vol. 48. no. 4. (pp456-67)

Fox, Geoff, and Mclay, John (2002) The Snicket Letters. *Books for Keeps* Vol. 134 (pp8-9): on-line: www.booksforkeeps.co.uk/245.

Franz, Marie-Louise von (1996) *The Interpretation of Fairy Tales.* 2nd, Revised Ed. London: Shambhala Publications

Ginsberg, Herbert and Cooper, Silvia (1979) *Piaget's Theory of Intellectual Development.* 2nd ed. Englewood Cliffs, NJ: Prentice-Hall Inc.

Gooderham, David (2003) Fantasizing It As It Is: Religious Language in Philip Pullman's Trilogy, His Dark Materials. *Children's Literature (ChLA Annual)* Vol. 31. (pp155-75)

Hunt, Peter (ed.) (1990) *Children's Literature: The Development of Criticism.* London: Routledge

Hunt, Peter (1992) *Literature for Children: Contemporary Criticism.* London: Routledge

Hunt, Peter (2005) *Understanding Children's Literature.* 2nd Ed. London: Routledge

Jung, C.G. (1968) *The Archetypes and the Collective Unconscious.* (Trans. R. F. C. Hull. The Collected Works of C.G. Jung. Ed. William McGuire. 2nd ed. Vol. 9, Part 1.) London: Routledge

Jung, C.G. (1991) *The Development of Personality.* (Trans. R.F.C. Hull. 5th Ed.) New York: Bollingen Foundation Inc. and Princeton University Press

Lenz, Millicent (2001) Philip Pullman. In Hunt, P. and Lenz, M. *Alternative Worlds in Fantasy Fiction.* London: Continuum, (pp122-69)

Nodelman, Perry (2000) Pleasure and Genre: Speculations on the Characteristics of Children's Fiction. *Children's Literature (ChLA Annual)*. Vol. 28. (pp1-14)

Pape, Walter (1992) Happy Endings in a World of Misery: A Literary Convention Between Social Constraints and Utopia in Children's and Adult Literature. *Poetics Today* Vol. 13, no. 1. (pp179-96)

Parsons, Wendy, and Nicholson, Catriona (1999) Talking to Philip Pullman: An Interview. *Lion and the Unicorn* Vol. 23, no. 1. (pp116-134)

Pickard, Phyllis M. (1961) *I Could A Tale Unfold: Violence, Horror and Sensationalism in Stories for Children*. London: Tavistock Publications

Poole, Richard (2001) Philip Pullman and the Republic of Heaven. *New Welsh Review*. Vol. 14, no.1 [53]. (pp15-22)

Pullman, Philip (1995) *Northern Lights*. London: Scholastic Children's Books

Pullman, Philip (1997) *The Subtle Knife*. London: Scholastic Children's Books

Pullman, Philip (2000) *The Amber Spyglass*. London: Scholastic Children's Books

Reynolds, Kimberley (2005) *Modern Children's Literature: An Introduction*. Basingstoke: Palgrave Macmillan

Rollin, Lucy and West, Mark I. (1999) *Psychoanalytic Responses to Children's Literature*. Jefferson, N.C.: McFarland

Rustin, Margaret, and Rustin, Michael (1987) *Narratives of Love and Loss: Studies in Modern Children's Fiction*. London: Verso

Snicket, Lemony (2001) *The Bad Beginning*. London: Egmont Books Ltd.

Snicket, Lemony (2001) *The Reptile Room*. London: Egmont Books Ltd.

Snicket, Lemony (2001) *The Wide Window*. London: Egmont Books Ltd.

Stallcup, Jackie E. (2002) Power, Fear and Children's Picture Books. *Children's Literature (ChLA Annual).* Vol. 30. (pp125-58)

Storr, Anthony (1998) *The Essential Jung: Selected Writings.* London: Fontana Press

Tucker, Nicholas (2003) *Darkness Visible: Inside the World of Philip Pullman.* Duxford: Wizard

Tucker, Nicholas (1992) Good Friends or Just Acquaintances?: The Relationship Between Child Psychology and Children's Literature. In Hunt, Peter (ed.) *Literature for Children: Contemporary Criticism.* London: Routledge, (pp156-73)

Tucker, Nicholas (1981) *The Child and the Book: A Psychological and Literary Exploration.* Cambridge: Cambridge University Press

Walsh, John (2002) Be Very Afraid. *The Independent* 3 Dec, on-line: http://enjoyment.independent.co.uk/books/features/article134354.ece.

Walter, Virginia A. (2000) Making Sense Out of Senselessness: The Social Construction of Adolescent Reality in the War Novels of Robert Westall. *Lion and the Unicorn* Vol. 24, no. 3. (pp432-44)

Warner, Marina (2005) Angels and Engines: The Culture of Apocalypse. *Raritan,* Vol. 25, No. 2. (pp12-41, 174)

Westall, Robert (1989) *Blitzcat.* London: Macmillan Children's Books

Winnicott, D. W. (1971) *Playing and Reality.* Harmondsworth: Penguin Books Ltd.

Zipes, Jack (1994) *Breaking the Magic Spell: Radical Theories of Folk and Fairy Tales.* 2nd ed. Lexington: The University Press of Kentucky

Zipes, Jack (1983) *Fairy Tales and the Art of Subversion: The Classic Genre for Children and the Process of Civilization.* London: Heinemann Educational Books Ltd.

Zipes, Jack (2002) *Sticks and Stones: The Troublesome Success of Children's Literature from Slovenly Peter to Harry Potter.* London: Routledge

Violets or Violence? Anarchism in Children's Literature

Ulf Schöne

Although children's literature seems an unlikely medium for a mostly abhorred and publicly discredited line of political thinking, anarchism, it can be found in texts, even before the incorporation of 'revolutionary' and 'alternative' topics in children's literature became popular in the 1970s. Allusions to anarchism are not always obvious, and hint at the alienation that defines the relationship between society and the individual. They pose questions about the persisting ideology of childhood and the cultural practices that come with the ideology. In short, such allusions to anarchism can be traced back to the hidden wounds that come with the making of a society.

Introduction

When anarchism as a political alternative received its deathblow in the wake of the Spanish Civil War, it had for some time been a waning ideological force. Although the movement seemed to have some momentum in its 'heyday between 1880 and 1914' (Sonn, 1992: 33-34), by the 1870s it had effectively lost the mandate for the revolutions-to-come to Marxism and consequently has been confined to the fringes of politics ever since. Nonetheless, the idea of anarchism has been a spectre haunting Europe. Where it could not be a political force it became a cultural one, and as such, left its traces in philosophy, literature and the arts. Modernist approaches to art, such as Dadaism, are deeply indebted to the creative inspiration that anarchistic thought and practice gave. Inventive writers, such as James Joyce and Ezra Pound, drew on anarchistic ideas in forming the concepts that influenced their works (Kadlec, 2000).

The aim of this paper is to show that anarchistic ideas have also left their impact on texts of a more conservative nature, namely those written for children and juveniles. Though children's literature seems an unlikely medium for a mostly abhorred and publicly discredited line of political thinking, the evidence suggests otherwise. Even before the incorporation of 'revolutionary' and 'alternative' topics in children's literature became popular in the era directly following the late 1960s, allusions to anarchism were put into texts addressed to younger audiences. These allusions are not always obvious; sometimes they appear disguised. This paper will briefly discuss the works of four authors to show possible modes of incorporating anarchistic ideas in children's literature.

Anarchism as a political force has always been separated into competing schools with a wide variety of beliefs. As a political theory, anarchism showed from its beginnings in the 19th Century a tendency to break up into different schools. Pierre-Joseph Proudhon, for instance, advocated anarchism based on an economic model, championing an ideal society built upon mutual help. In contrast, his contemporary Max Stirner denounced society as a whole. For him, it was only acceptable as long as it met the self-interest of the individual. Further, Michael Bakunin's conviction that a free society was to be achieved by revolutionary means was not in favour with all anarchists.

So as not to be overwhelmed by all of these differences, the reader can take as a guideline one point upon which all anarchists would have agreed. The term anarchism can be traced back to the Greek "an-arche", which, when translated, means "without rule". Freedom from all forms of authority, therefore, is the common ground from which all ventures into anarchist theory have started.

T.H. White's The Sword in the Stone

The Sword in the Stone (1958), the first part of T.H. White's King Arthur adaptation, here discussed in the version, The Once and Future King tetralogy, represents an example of a juvenile novel that openly shows a sympathetic attitude towards anarchism. The novel covers the childhood years of 'the Wart' up to his coronation as King Arthur, presented through a landscape of 'Olde England' nostalgia and fantastic adventures. However, at its core, it is a novel about Wart's education. Wart's teacher is the sorcerer Merlyn who tries to prepare the boy for his future task by occasionally allowing him to take the form of various animals. The intention of this rather droll educational programme is to give him insight into the problem of 'might', a problem that will be central for his future rule as king. In turn, Wart is transformed into a fish, a hawk, an ant, a wild goose and a badger. At least four of these educational episodes deal not only with might in general, but with its political organisation.

In fish-form, Wart is sent to meet 'the old despot' (White, 1987: 49) of the moat, a pike. The monarch gives him an outline of his political philosophy:

> "There is nothing ...except the power which you pretend to seek: power to grind and power to digest, power to seek and power to find, power to await and power to claim, all power and pitilessness springing from the nape of your neck". (p50)

For him, as the ruler, 'only Might is Right' (p50), a sentiment that clearly does not win the sympathy of Wart: 'The Wart thought for himself that he did not care for Mr. P.' (p50). From this primal political organisation, the curriculum shifts to a more sophisticated one, as the boy spends a night in the mews as a hawk to experience the 'Spartan military mess' (p75) of the falcons. Here he learns about the harsh regime of the warrior aristocracy, with its rituals and emphasis on honour and deportment. Later, as an ant, Wart is cast into a totalitarian society. The political organisation of the ants is presented as an amalgamation of fascism and communism, with the emmets singing "'Antland, Antland, Over All'" (p126) in wartime.

At the end of each of these episodes, Wart's life is endangered in some way. He is almost eaten by the pike, nearly dies in the initiation ritual of the hawks, and well-nigh perishes in the war of the ants. The tranquillity of the fourth educational episode stands in stark contrast to the violent endings of the former ones. In the shape of a goose he is allowed to experience the peaceful company of the wild geese. The reasons for their peacefulness are explained by one of the geese:

> She told him how every Whitefront was an individual - not governed by laws or leaders, except when they came about spontaneously. They had no kings like Uther, no laws like the bitter Norman ones. They did not own things in common. Any goose who found something nice to eat considered it his own and would peck any other who tried to thieve it. At the same time no goose claimed any exclusive territorial right in any part of the world - except its nest, and that was private property. (p169)

This libertarian society resembles anarchy with a Proudhonian tint, in that it allows for private property and builds upon the geese helping each other out on their voyages. That it is to be understood as a model for man becomes evident when one considers the warm tone of the episode, and its non-violent end. The political organisation of the geese succeeds where the organisations of the other animals fail, namely in finding a solution to the problem of might. This is highlighted in the following and final episode that serves to sum up the lessons learned previously. In a dialogue with the badger, the solution to the problem of might and the question of how to overcome war is broken down to a formula: where there are no boundaries, there are no wars. That leads back to the anarchistic organisation of the wild geese, for by definition they have no use for borders. "'There are no boundaries among geese. ...How can you have boundaries if you fly?'" (p168) Thus, although the 'A-word' is missing, the novel is in parts an open propagation of anarchism, albeit not a very agitative form; instead rather romantic. This reading becomes even more evident if one considers the posthumously published sequel *The Book of Merlyn* (1977), which openly advocates anarchism as a remedy to war.

Michael de Larrabeiti's *The Borribles*

In the first part of Michael de Larrabeiti's Borribles trilogy, the concept of anarchism and its function in the narrative are different from those in *The Sword in the Stone*. The allusions to anarchism are nevertheless equally visible.

Anarchistic ideas are prominent in the way of life of the Borribles presented in the first pages of the novel. As the reader is told, Borribles dwell in urban surroundings and in the undergrounds of cities. Though their appearance is childlike, they are not children, for 'as long as a Borrible remains at liberty he or she will never age' (De Larrabeiti, 2005: 4). If they are caught by the police and their long pointed ears are clipped, they will 'grow into a malevolent and adventureless adulthood' (p5) and cease to be Borribles. They despise money and want no dealings with it:

> So Borribles are outcasts, but unlike most outcasts they enjoy themselves and wouldn't be anything else. They delight in feeling independent and it is this feeling that is most important to them. Consequently they have no real leaders, though some may rise into prominence from time to time, but on the whole they manage without authority. (p5)

While de Larrabeiti's description of anarchism resembles White's in the sense that it is depicted with sympathy and thus presented as something desirable, the differences between the two visions are more interesting. The anarchy of the Borribles is fenced, secluded; it is opposed to a reactionary outside world. Their anarchy is one of a day-to-day struggle to preserve it, while White's is a utopian all-embracing one, where man stops being troubled by might.

156

In fact, anarchy in *The Borribles* is a narrative device. The fight for its preservation motivates the plot; to protect their libertarian life-style, the Borribles start a terrorist attack on the rat-like Rumbles, whom they suspect of trying to colonise their turf. In a twist which emphasizes the underlining anarchistic morals of the novel, the Rumbles never intended such a course of action; in fact, the real threat to the liberty-loving Borribles lurks amidst their own ranks, in the form of the despot Flinthead and the schemer Spiff. This echoes the sentiment of more pessimistic anarchists; vigilance and mistrust are the basis of an anarchistic life. This sentiment is adequately framed by the novel's dystopian depiction of urban decay and its rough language and brutality, the latter being apparent in sentences such as 'Five stones arriving like bullets on a kneecap are as effective as amputation.' (p86)

The Borribles (1976) can be read as a story about the struggle to live on one's own terms in an estranged world, and about corruption through leadership. Though it is less an outright propagation of anarchism than *The Sword in the Stone*, it is reminiscent of a fable for the urban anarchist guerrilla. Its ideological lure lies in making the self-preservation of the anarchist-egoist seem attractive. This outlook on anarchism corresponds with the general tendencies of the movement in the 1970s in that it refrains from challenging the state through direct action and instead tries to carve out a niche of its own. It thus exists 'side by side with, and in spite of, the dominant authoritarian trends of our society' (Ward, 1973: 11). The anarchist Colin Ward strikingly exemplifies the stance and hopes which inform these politics with a quote from his predecessor, Gustav Landauer:

> The state is not something which can be destroyed by a revolution, but is a condition, a certain relationship between human beings, a mode of human behaviour; we destroy it by contracting other relationships, by behaving differently. (p19)

Joachim Ringelnatz's Geheimes Kinder-Spiel-Buch and Kinder-Verwirr-Buch

The possible link to anarchism can sometimes become visible when taking into account the context of the writings, as in the case of Joachim Ringelnatz's unconventional children's books, published in the cultural and ideological turmoil of the Weimar Republic. The content of *Geheimes Kinder-Spiel-Buch* (the secret child games book) and the *Kinder-Verwirr-Buch* (the book for confusing children) is very controversial. Being threatened with penalties, the publisher had to paste over the age-reference "for children from five to fifteen" on the jacket of the *Geheimes Kinder-Spiel-Buch*. Instead, a warning was to be placed on the cover, stating that this was a book for adults only. A critical account of this incident is given by Robert Gernhard (2000: 59-66).

The content which caused such controversy was a collection of children's rhymes. Harmless in form, the games they suggest are often more problematic. Some, like the "African Duel", would neither cause harm to the child nor the inventory of the (bourgeois) household, but most of the games are potentially destructive. The game entitled "How to invent something. Only for children with guts" encourages the reader to lay a dead fish and other objects on the keys of a piano, and then to add hydrochloric acid and glowing coals. Every game concludes with some advice to the child on how to react if s/he faces punishment from parents for playing the game. In the case of the invention game the author has quite a drastic suggestion:

> And if your parents want to punish you,
> put defiantly your hands into the glowing coals
> and just curtly say
> that they should get themselves buried real quick.
> (Ringelnatz, 1985: 20)

Some of the poems in the *Kinder-Verwirr-Buch* pick up this trait of defiance towards parents. In "To Berlin children" parents are decried as drunken and gambling sodomites. Another poem propagates the forming of gangs:

> Children, you have to be more daring!
> You allow grown-ups to lie to you
> and beat you. - Just think about it: Five children are enough
> to give Grandma a beating.
> (Ringelnatz, 1931: 36)

Combined with some silly, disrespectful and downright ugly drawings by the author, one can be excused if the first reaction to these books is one of confusion.

One could argue that the texts belong to the tradition of nonsense literature and can therefore avoid any awkward questions which their being described as children's literature might pose. However, according to Jean-Jacques Lecercle, nonsense is defined by its contradictions, it

> ...is on the whole a conservative-revolutionary genre. It is conservative because deeply respectful of authority in all forms: rules of grammar, maxims of conversation and of politeness [...]. It is

> inextricably mixed with the other aspect, for which the genre is justly famous, the liberated, light-fantastic, nonsensical aspect of nonsense, where rules and maxims appear joyously subverted. (Lecercle, 1994: 2-3)

Nonsense, then, in the end is an affirmation of the order it playfully disturbs. In contrast, the order being disturbed in the texts of Ringelnatz, namely the hierarchy of the child-parent relationship, cannot be reconciled in the light of the challenges posed by the poems. The defining feature of the texts is that they indulge in insurgence against parental authority. They have a revolutionary edge to them, but at the same time are missing the pronounced conservative element of nonsense literature.

Further, the texts do not fully adhere to a 'carnivalistic' tradition; though they celebrate the upheaval of the natural order of things as far as family life is concerned, their 'turning the world on its head' goes only half way. While playing, the child may affront the norms of the parents, but the texts make clear that such actions will not be allowed to go unpunished. The games suggested are never empowering; the exemption from punishment inherent to the carnival cannot be found here. The texts therefore share some of the characteristics of nonsense and carnival, but not enough to make them representative of these traditions.

The books can be said to have anarchistic potential on three different levels. They unmask the relationship between generations as a despotic one based upon violence. It is an affirmation of just how powerless the children are in that it takes five of them to retaliate against a grandmother. Moreover, the combination of silliness and wickedness makes the books harder to attack; by eluding any acknowledged categories of literary practice, they sneak under the radar of public discourse. Finally, the publishing of these texts is in itself an anarchistic act since it is an affront to the prevailing bourgeois value system, something the authorities were clearly aware of, judging by the legal actions against the publisher.

Tove Jansson's Moomin books

Unlike the previous examples, the incorporation of anarchistic ideas may seem less obvious at first glance in the case of Tove Jansson's Moomin books. One critic labelled the social structure of the Moomin valley as a form of 'soft anarchism' (Orlov, 1993: 27) while another characterised it as 'petty bourgeois' (Mattenklott, 1994: 92). The latter initially appears more plausible when one considers the tranquil and gentle family life that the Moomins display.

Nonetheless, some aspects of the texts back up the anarchism thesis. The character Snufkin, for example, shows a decidedly anti-authoritarian trait, which becomes most obvious in his defiance of the park keeper in *Moominsummer Madness* (1954): 'All of his life Snufkin had yearned to tear down signs forbidding him everything he was fond of [...]' (Jansson, 1969: 78). Additionally, money and a governmental organisation play no role whatsoever in the later Moomin books.

However, what finally tips the scale in favour of an ideological reading is the celebration of extreme individualism which one finds in characters like Little My, Mymble and the afore-mentioned Snufkin. Loneliness is often described in sympathetic tones, as 'mild and exquisite' (Jansson, 1971: 5), and a recurring theme of the Moomin novels is the longing for loneliness. These preferences come at the cost of a certain reserved attitude towards society:

> There is nothing better than to have a good time, and nothing is easier to accomplish. Mymble didn't feel pity for those who she met and soon afterwards forgot, and she never tried to get involved in their doings. (p55)

For the freedom loving Snufkin, the sight of a crammed settlement leads to a sensation of anxiety, a feeling which he seeks relief from in a telling exclamation: "Oh, all you houses, how I dislike you!" (p10)

Freedom in the Moomin novels is the freedom from community other than the one voluntarily sought. This represents an escapist vision of society, a flowery egoist Elysium, where everyone can in principle live according to his or her own liking and where material and social needs are met nonetheless. Its serenity and peacefulness resemble the anarchy of White's geese.

Max Stirner, the central proponent of the individualist streak of anarchist thinking, advocated a 'Verein von Egoisten' (Stirner, 1924: 178), a union of egoists, an assembly of autonomous individuals with the sole purpose to serve the self-interest of its affiliates. According to Stirner, as soon as there were no more benefits to be reaped from such a community for the 'ego', the person in question would naturally leave and find another union that better served his or her purposes. While it is debatable as to whether the ideal society of the Moomin valley can be described as a 'union of egoists' in the spirit of Stirner, the pronounced feeling for individuality which is expressed does bear a resemblance to the philosophy of egoism, in the same way as it represents the primal cell for all anarchistic strivings.

Conclusion

As these examples suggest, anarchism can indeed play a role in literary texts for children and the modes in which the anarchistic influence is present can vary considerably. One does not necessarily have to understand all of these ventures into the realm of anarchism as part of an original political discourse. Although this is clearly the case with T.H. White's animal fables in *The Once and Future King*, it seems unlikely in the case of Tove Jansson. However it is not the presence of a political affiliation which makes these texts ideological and thus a highly interesting field of research for a scholar of children's literature.

What all of the aforementioned works have in common is that their narratives promote the 'organisation' of societies which are very different to those existing in the real world. They therefore cast a shadow of doubt on the latter and point to their failings. In their resistance to comment constructively on existing power relationships and their promotion of the downright antithesis of these relationships, the fundamental condition of modern human man becomes apparent: the irreconcilable opposition between the individual on the one hand and society, in its many emanations and with its many power-enforcing agents, on the other.

The descriptions of an alternative way of life may be utopian (White), rebellious (de Larrabeiti), destructive (Ringelnatz) or escapist (Jansson), but they all contain a feeling of dissatisfaction with the status quo and a longing for the unreal, which in itself is highly political. Children's literature has always been a tool for the socialisation of the child. These texts not only reject this role, they also denounce socialisation itself and point to the space that it left. Their refusal to pay tribute to the accomplishments of societal organisations can be seen as an indication of the friction that accompanies the experience of socialisation.

These texts, then, hint at the alienation that defines the relationship between society and the individual. They pose questions about the persisting ideology of childhood and the cultural practices that come with this ideology. In short, their allusions to anarchism can be traced back to the hidden wounds that come with the making of a society.

Anarchism has always been more than a mere political theory; for its advocates, it was 'a faith, and a way of life' that has a 'powerful hold over the imagination' (Sonn, 1992: pXIII). As such, it is inevitable that it leaves deep traces, and, as shown in this paper, it is no coincidence that it does so in children's literature. As such, it once more becomes apparent that research into children's literature is often first and foremost a research into the 'backyards' of society.

Note
1. English quotes referring to non-English texts are translations made by the author of this article.

Bibliography
Gernhard, Robert (2000) So ihr nicht werdet wie die Kinder. Die Kinderbücher des Joachim Ringelnatz. *Text + Kritik*, no. 148. (pp59-66)

Jansson, Tove (1954) *Farlig midsommar.* Stockholm: Norstedts Förlag

Jansson, Tove (1971) *Sent i november.* Stockholm: Norstedts Förlag

Kadlec, David (2002) *Mosaic Modernism.* Baltimore: John Hopkins University Press

Larrabeiti, Michael de (1976) *The Borribles.* London: Bodley Head

Lecercle, Jean-Jacques (1994) *Philosophy of Nonsense: The Intuitions of Victorian Nonsense Literature.* London: Routledge

Mattenklott, Gundel (1994) *Zauberkreide. Kinderliteratur seit 1945.* Frankfurt am Main: Fischer

Orlov, Janina (1993) Mumin on my mind. *Horisont*, no. 40. (pp24-34)

Ringelnatz, Joachim (1931) *Kinder-Verwirr-Buch.* Berlin: Ernst Rowohlt Verlag

Ringelnatz, Joachim (1924) *Geheimes Kinder-Spiel-Buch.* Berlin: Eulenspiegel Verlag

Sonn, Richard D. (1992) *Anarchism.* New York: Twayne Publishers

Stirner, Max (1844) *Der Einzige und sein Eigentum.* Berlin: Rothgiesser & Possekiel

Ward, Colin (1973) *Anarchy in Action*. London: Harper & Row

White, T.H. (1958) *The Once and Future King*. London: Collins

An Invitation to Explore: David Almond's Early Children's Texts and the Adolescent Reader

Liz Thiel

Almond's early stories are characterised by a postmodern indeterminacy that resists absolutes and firmly sites the reader as interpreter. The adolescent reader who engages with their philosophical and critical complexities is unlikely to remain unchanged by the experience.

In his Carnegie Medal acceptance speech for *Skellig*, David Almond proposed the notion of 'a Blakean garden in every school, where children and their teachers [could] simply wander, explore and dream.' His plea was for respite from the 'noses-to-the-grindstone treadmill' style of contemporary education and was simultaneously a validation of the 'inspirational' teachers, the supposed 'heretics', who recognised that children must sometimes 'be left alone, given space and silence and respect' (Almond, 1999: 2). Former teacher Almond is still something of an educator, albeit one allied to the 'heretical' school of instruction. Read in chronological sequence and considered sequentially, his three early children's texts - *Skellig* (1998), *Kit's Wilderness* (1999) and *Heaven Eyes* (2000) - are a progressive introduction to both philosophical and critical thought, each subsequent novel offering a greater space in which minds can wander and explore. Although the stories are underpinned, to varying degrees, by a Blakean ethos of free thinking and heightened perception, they are characterised by a postmodern indeterminacy that resists absolutes and firmly sites the reader as interpreter. There is no definitive explanation of events, and Almond's frequently bemused narrators are of limited assistance. The reader is essentially 'left alone' to consider the potential meanings of Almond's dream-like tales and, ultimately perhaps, to wonder about the very nature of story and of the literary text itself.

As tales marketed for an 11 to 13 plus readership - according to Hodder Children's Books - *Skellig*, *Kit's Wilderness* and *Heaven Eyes* would seem to be eminently suited to the adolescent - or precociously adolescent - mind. According to Joseph Appleyard, 'The adolescent reader is entering the foothills of [a] whole new range of thought [about the meaning of a text]' and developing the ability to 'think about thinking, to reflect critically about one's own thoughts' (1994: 113, 97), and Almond's stories, examined in sequence, enable a gradual progression into increasingly complex philosophical and critical thought.

Skellig is a profound yet intensely simple tale that disputes the boundaries of given reality. *Kit's Wilderness* explores the interplay between past and present and the power of the imagination on a journey through 'the caves and tunnels in our heads' (p215), while *Heaven Eyes*, perhaps the most challenging of the three, focuses on the concept of truth and the ambiguities of the literary text. These are tales that seemingly disregard adult expectations of children's literature: the issues they raise are as fundamental to an adult as to an adolescent. Yet if there is a concession towards an adolescent audience, apart from the young age of the novels' protagonists, it would appear to lie in Almond's narrative style. His stories avoid the confrontational stance that is often characteristic of adult postmodern texts. There is no sense of antagonism between reader and narrative, no imperative to delve below the superficial storyline, which is perhaps why his novels can also be enjoyed by younger readers. But if the adolescent chooses to experiment and to exercise her developing ability for critical reflection, than *Skellig*, *Kit's Wilderness* and *Heaven Eyes* might be perceived as metaphorical doorways that can lead to revised perceptions.

Doors and doorways are a conspicuous feature of *Skellig*, *Kit's Wilderness* and *Heaven Eyes*, and Almond's repeated use of them to signify entrance into alternative realities is one of several motifs and assertions that proclaim his allegiance to Blake. Michael discovers Skellig by passing through an old door that 'creaked and cracked' (p6), and he and Mina unlock the door of a boarded-up house to help in Skellig's regeneration (p82); in *Kit's Wilderness*, Askew's den is accessed by removing 'old doors slung across it' (p5); Erin, January and Mouse of *Heaven Eyes* sail away on a homemade raft constructed from 'three doors laid flat and nailed down on to planks' (p33). Perhaps symbolically representative of Blake's 'doors of perception' that, if they were cleansed, would allow 'everything [to] appear...as it is: infinite' (Blake, 1975: 14), Almond's doors are also agents of change. The 'danger' signs that appear implicitly or explicitly across them - the 'danger' sign on the garage door in *Skellig*, the 'keep out' signs on the boards covering the drift mine in *Kit's Wilderness* and the raft doors emblazoned with 'entrance danger exit' in *Heaven Eyes* - are warnings of disruption, but in Almond, as in Blake, disruption is productive, leading to a revised consciousness for Michael, Kit and Erin. This is the Blakean dialectic in simple form; Almond's protagonists pass from innocence and limited vision to experience, and so to a state of higher perception. It is appropriate, and perhaps not entirely coincidental, that while Blake saw 'angels in the trees as a boy and listened to the voices of "Messengers from Heaven" ' (Marshall, 1994: 1), Almond's first children's novel should feature a boy who finds an angel in the garage of his home.

The first novel, *Skellig* - winner of the 1998 Whitbread Children's Book of the Year and the Carnegie Medal - might be deemed an introduction to the philosophical and critical emphasis that prevails throughout Almond's work. Thematically less dense than Almond's subsequent texts, but similarly concerned with the development of new perceptions, *Skellig* is challenging but accessible, inviting the reader to consider that 'an extraordinary being' (p76) may exist in tandem with the everyday and that by 'listen[ing] to the deepest, deepest places of the dark' (p108), the human mind can reclaim a sense of its diminished primal spirituality and innate perceptiveness. There are Wordsworthian resonances throughout the text, but most noticeably in Almond's characterisation of Michael's baby sister; recently arrived but close to death, she epitomises the new-born of the 'Intimations of Immortality' ode who possesses the radiance and awareness of a Heavenly pre-existence: 'She looked right into me, right into the place where all my dreams were, and she smiled', recounts Michael (p168). In addition, *Skellig* is rich in Blakean references. But while Mina's comments about schooling and the potential ossification of the mind - ' The mind needs to be opened out to the world, not shuttered inside a gloomy classroom ... [it] becomes inflexible. It stops thinking and imagining' (pp47, 74) - are pure Blakean philosophy, they also function as a guide towards exploratory thought. Only by 'opening out' her mind can the reader accept *Skellig* for anything other than a fantasy tale; only by remaining, or becoming, flexible and by questioning the concepts of dream and reality can the reader begin to comprehend the possibilities that may lie beyond the given 'norm.'

Ultimately, she must do so alone. Almond denies his reader the comfort of a traditional closure by refusing to acknowledge absolutes; only the reader can decide whether Skellig is reality or dream, whether the two are interchangeable, or are, perhaps, the same. Neither Michael nor Mina offers a definitive answer. Mina concedes that 'truth and dreams are always getting muddled' (p49) and Michael confesses that even if he and Mina *were* dreaming 'we wouldn't know' (p79). Like Mum's story about shoulder blades - 'They say [they] are where your wings were, when you were an angel...where your wings will grow again one day' (p36) - *Skellig* may be merely 'a fairy tale for little kids' (p36). Perhaps the story is a dream prompted by Michael's experience of the near death of his baby sister. Or perhaps the question of fact or fantasy is unimportant. The emphasis of Almond's tale would seem to lie in its celebration of the possible and of the heightened perception that

Michael and Mina achieve by following Blakean advice to 'open [their] eyes a little wider, look a little harder' (p122). Moreover, theirs would seem to be a state of consciousness available to all. Mina's belief that 'we have to be ready to move forward' and that 'maybe this is not how we are meant to be forever' (p94), suggests that within everyone lies the possibility of greater spiritual awareness and development and that much can be gained by imagining beyond the limits of prescribed reality. These are substantial philosophical issues presented coherently in story form and as such provide an accessible foundation for further critical thought. There may be gaps in the narrative but they are purposeful spaces in which the reader can reflect, consciously and self-critically, as she attempts to comprehend and respond to the implications of the text.

Full comprehension is clearly not an issue for Almond. As Mina says, 'Sometimes we think we should be able to know everything. But we can't. We have to allow ourselves to see what there is to see and we have to imagine' (p131). However, greater perception would seem to be more easily accessed through artistic imagination. Mina believes that 'drawing makes you look at the world more closely. It helps you to see what you're looking at more clearly' (p24), and Michael notices that 'the more I drew, the more my hand and arm became free' (p126). Furthermore, Almond proposes in *Skellig,* but more overtly in his second novel, *Kit's Wilderness*, that artistic imagination and stories, visual and textual, possess powerful and influential properties. Michael dreams of Skellig with his sick sister (p104), draws Skellig at the door of his baby sister's hospital ward (p127) and his mother dreams that Skellig and the baby dance together (p150). Kit, in *Kit's Wilderness*, writes a story about the Ice Age boy, Lak, and brings about change within his present-day world. Both *Skellig* and *Kit's Wilderness* focus on the concept of reality, but *Kit's Wilderness* is clearly more philosophically demanding. Although each text is concerned with exploring notions of the real, *Kit's Wilderness* also contemplates the possibility that imaginative story itself is as real as the tangible, visible world.

To approach an adolescent reader with the suggestion that story is a form of reality might be to invite confusion, although as Peter Hollindale states, 'the adolescent novel of ideas requires (and finds) not less but more intelligence in its young readers than previous generations would have expected' (1996: 319). Nevertheless, it is a problematic concept whatever the age of the reader, and consequently the novel treads gently, exploring the idea of reality in different ways before broaching the potential complexities of story. Kit is unaware of the other realities that surround him - 'I watched, saw nothing else. Just the kids, the wilderness, the river' (p13) - until his experience with the Game of Death opens his eyes, although at first he must squint in order to see the 'skinny bodies in the flickering light' (p50). His journey into the alternative reality of the 'caves and tunnels in his head' (p215) via the Game of Death in which participants are chosen by the turning of a knife, is both frightening and compelling - 'I was terrified that the knife would point at me... But I also wanted it. I was driven to it' (p48). However, he survives, understanding at last that reality is comprised of both past and present and that although the past continues to survive within memory, and is his legacy, he belongs within the reality of the present. This idea alone might be considered sufficiently difficult for a young reader, but to perceive *Kit's Wilderness* purely in this way is to oversimplify. While reality in *Kit's Wilderness* exists in the past and present, it would also seem to exist in Kit's ostensibly imaginary tale of Lak. Kit's story about the Ice Age boy takes solid form, its characters interact with and become a tangible part of the alternative, co-existent reality that Kit experiences in the drift mine with Askew: 'Then [Lak's] mother released her son and came to me....She took my hand...She touched my cheek' (p203). Once again, as in *Skellig*, Almond focuses on the notion that what is perceived as imaginary, or dream, is fused with reality but also suggests that the artist/writer, through imagination, has the power to influence the supposedly real world. Allie tells Kit that 'you can change the world and keep on changing it', and he nods. 'I knew that from my stories and my dreams', he says (p137).

This apparently inextricable relationship between the imaginary and real in which one can influence the other might be interpreted as a perfect, seamless blending of inner and outer worlds. Ted Hughes asserts that, in great artistic works, 'the full presence of the inner world combines with and is reconciled to the full presence of the outer world' and that this is the essence of the great artist's imagination (1976: 92). It may be that *Kit's Wilderness* hints at such a potential state. The imaginative and supposedly real worlds of Kit's experience come together and a new world emerges in which given reality (the outer world) and imagination (the inner world) are allotted equal status and become, temporarily, one and the same. Kit, Askew, Lak and his mother co-exist within the same space and affect each other; Kit receives 'brightly-coloured pebbles' from Lak's mother (p203) and restores her son, and all is resolved. To conceive of imagination and reality as conjoined is a difficult philosophical concept that is arguably beyond the grasp of an adolescent, but whether it is truly comprehensible, either by adolescent or adult, is largely irrelevant. The nature of philosophy is such that there are rarely definitive answers, and, as Geoff Moss suggests, 'perhaps provocation is as important as satisfaction for children' (1992: 51). If the adolescent reader of *Kit's Wilderness* is provoked into wondering whether the novel is more than a magical ghost story - although it can be read as such - then the relationship between the imaginary and the real is perhaps the most complex issue to arise from Almond's text. *Kit's Wilderness* fails to offer a full explanation of events; indeed, such complexity may defy articulation. It is left to the reader to contemplate the possible meanings of the tale and to reach her own conclusions.

Almond's third novel, *Heaven Eyes*, might be viewed as a complementary and progressive sequel to his earlier work. The same train of philosophical thought common to *Skellig* and *Kit's Wilderness* prevails; *Heaven Eyes* explores different co-existent realities, the relationship between the imaginary and the real, and the power of story. The alternative reality of the Black Middens and the printing works is juxtaposed against the given reality that is Whitegates, and central character Erin achieves a revised perception by the time her journey concludes. Yet the emphasis of this third book clearly moves away from that of its predecessors to focus on the text itself. Although Almond's earlier novels display a postmodern indeterminacy that resists absolutes, *Heaven Eyes* could be construed as an archetypal postmodern text. Intertextual and replete with ambiguity, *Heaven Eyes* not only offers no absolutes on which the reader can depend, but questions their very existence. There is, ultimately, only story. And while Almond's text may celebrate the interrelatedness of individual experience and personal stories - 'our stories mix and mingle like the twisting currents of a river' (p214) - it simultaneously suggests that the truth of story is subjective and that it may simply be the product of interpretation.

The question of truth is not an issue in Almond's earlier texts; the emphasis is on the broader implications of Michael and Kit's experiences. However, *Heaven Eyes* foregrounds the concept of truth in its opening page and so immediately calls the reader's attention to the text's potential veracity - or fictionality. Erin's opening speech is a plea for credibility: 'Some people will tell you that none of these things happened...But they did happen....People will tell you that this is not Heaven Eyes...But...look at her...Listen to her strange sweet voice...Everything is true. So listen' (p3). The vehemence of her request and her direct address to the reader have an adverse effect; it may be that she protests too much. Moreover, the fact the she and her friends are supposedly 'damaged children' (p3), a comment that immediately succeeds her opening plea, invites the reader to question her credibility still further. Erin's narrative may derive from wishful thinking and a desire to escape from a shuttered, hopeless existence into 'the Paradise that we'd all lost' (p5). In her eyes, at least, her experience teaches her to love 'being alive, being me, in this world, here and now' (p208) and to wonder at 'the most astounding things that can lie waiting as each day dawns' (p215). But her interpretation of events would seem to be entirely subjective; the reliability of her perception is frequently and disruptively undermined by the ambiguities, both inherent and intertextual, of the text.

To critically appraise a novel and probe for alternative meanings might be seen as the work of the practised literary critic rather than the young reader, but the gaps and contradictions in Almond's texts are such that they invite speculation, particularly for the more widely-read adolescent. January's tale of his mother would seem to be based on sentimental melodrama rather than actuality: 'He told the story of a frantic woman in a stormy winter night' (p6). Mouse believes in the love of a father who tattooed 'Please look after me' on his young son's skin in a parody of the Paddington Bear tales (pp8, 77). The children's journey to the Black Middens parallels a trip to the underworld of Greek legend; Mouse pays January, the ferryman, to take him aboard: 'He held out the five-pence piece..."Go on", said Mouse. "Take it. Please. It'll be my fare " ' (p37). Furthermore, Heaven Eyes herself is reminiscent of Gollum from *The Hobbit* and *The Lord of the Rings*. With her webbed toes and fingers, her 'moon-round, watery-blue' eyes (p51), she lives in the "underworld" of the Black Middens and the printing works as Gollum resides beneath the earth, and speaks of her 'treasures' as Gollum speaks of his 'precious', in a language that is as peculiar as his own. Tempting the children with chocolates that are 'the sweetest thing of all' (p76) in the manner of a fairytale witch, she is a supposed innocent who 'sees through all the grief and trouble in the world to the Heaven that does lie beneath' (p69). Yet she seemingly is ignorant of the world beyond the Black Middens and speaks casually of Grampa having 'fettled' the ghosts who came too near (p83). It may be that Heaven Eyes is truly a beautiful innocent, that the children do find a saint in the mud and that Erin's mother speaks and comforts her from beyond the grave. But the ambiguity of Almond's narrative, its intertextual playfulness and the alternative readings that are freely available, continually suggest that all is not as it seems.

In this way, *Heaven Eyes* suggests that the literary text can, and often does, play games with its reader. It is a notion that can prove disturbing; as Appleyard points out, 'growth does not always feel comfortable when it is happening' (p110). However, if *Heaven Eyes* invites a response that is more commonly expected from older readers - 'a response that does not take the story for granted...but sees it as a text that someone has made, as something problematic and therefore demanding interpretation' (Appleyard, 1991: 121) - it does so with apparent respect for the age and experience of its reader. Its ambiguities are clear and await discovery; indeed, *Heaven Eyes* might be considered an appropriate introduction to the duplicitous nature of the postmodern literary text and to the alternative readings that are frequently available within them. Like Almond's other children's texts, it offers no absolutes but, rather, presents possibilities for contemplation. There is no overt ideology, other than that of potentiality; the reader is free to respond to the text in her own way and to do with it what she will.

This freedom for the reader would seem to be Almond's primary agenda throughout his children's texts; each novel offers an ever-greater space for contemplation as it confronts increasingly complex issues. Questions about the boundaries of reality in *Skellig* are reinforced and supplemented by notions about the reality of past, present and of story itself in *Kit's Wilderness*. *Heaven Eyes* continues the preoccupation with reality but draws attention to the nature of the text, to the concept that truth may be merely interpretation. While each text can be approached individually, they together provide a cumulative, accessible foundation for philosophical and critical thought and invite the reader to take part. There is no sense of overt didacticism; Almond's teaching would seem to be strictly of the "heretical" variety. And although he might be criticised for imposing traditionally comforting conclusions on his young reader - Michael, Kit and Erin anticipate more positive futures as a result of their experiences - this is less of a concession to children's literature than to the nature of the Blakean philosophy inherent to each text. Increased perception, as Blake asserts, engenders freedom and only by 'melting apparent surfaces' away (p14) can man achieve his full potential. Having perceived the alternative realities that lie beneath the surface of their existence, Michael, Kit and Erin are empowered and achieve the potential to move forward.

Movement forward, for both characters and reader, would seem to be fundamental to Almond's scheme. The adolescent reader of his texts who engages with their philosophical and critical complexities is unlikely to remain unchanged by the experience. As Wolfgang Iser states, 'the production of the meaning of literary texts...entails the possibility that we may formulate ourselves' (1980: 68), and it may be that the reader, like the central characters of *Skellig*, *Kit's Wilderness* and *Heaven Eyes*, undergoes change and similarly achieves a revised consciousness. Having been largely 'left alone' to consider the potential meanings of Almond's tales and to assume the role of interpreter, the reader has only her own intellect on which to depend. She can choose to read Almond's texts as fantasy, or can opt to fully engage with their complexities and allow herself to be drawn into deeper speculations. There is no compunction for her to do so. However, as Ricoeur states, narrative offers us '...the freedom to conceive of the world in new ways' (cited in Appleyard, 1994: 19) and the adolescent, possessed of a developing ability to 'think about thinking' (p97) is perfectly situated to question her preconceptions and to look again at the world in which she lives. Betsy Hearne, writing of Virginia Hamilton in *Twentieth Century Children's Writers*, comments, 'With plenty of books that fit easily, there must be that occasional book that grows the mind a size larger' (cited in Hollindale, 1996: 317). While Almond's *Skellig, Kit's Wilderness* and *Heaven Eyes* are primarily spaces in which the reader can wander and explore, there is, within each of them, an implicit invitation for such growth.

Bibliography

Almond, David. (1998) *Skellig.* London: Hodder Children's Books

Almond, David. (1999) *Kit's Wilderness.* London: Hodder Children's Books

Almond, David. (2000) *Heaven Eyes.* London: Hodder Children's Books

Almond, David. (1999) David Almond's 1999 Carnegie Medal Acceptance Speech. *Youth Library Review*, no. 27. Youth Library Review website
Available: http://www.la-hq.org.uk/groups/ylg/archive/ylr27_htm.
Accessed June 2000.

Appleyard, Joseph A. (1991) *Becoming a Reader: The Experience of Fiction from Childhood to Adulthood.* Cambridge: Cambridge University Press

Blake, William. (1975) *The Marriage of Heaven and Hell.* Oxford: Oxford University Press

Hollindale, Peter (1996) The Adolescent Novel of Ideas. In Egoff, Sheila et al (eds.) *Only Connect: Readings on Children's Literature.* Oxford: Oxford University Press

Hughes, Ted (1976) Myth and Education. In Fox, Geoff et al (eds.) *Writers, Critics and Children: Articles from Children's Literature in Education*. London: Heinemann Educational.

Iser, Wolfgang (1980) The Reading Process: A Phenomenological Approach. In *Reader-Response Criticism: From Formalism to Post-structuralism*. London: John Hopkins University Press

Marshall, Peter (1994) *William Blake: Visionary Anarchist*. London: Freedom Press

Moss, Geoff (1992) Metafiction, Illustration and the Poetics of Children's Literature. In Hunt, Peter (ed) *Literature for Children: Contemporary Criticism*. London: Routledge

Author Biographies

Noga Applebaum is in the final year of a PhD in Children's Literature at Roehampton University, London. Her dissertation engages with representations of technology in contemporary science fiction written for children and young adults. She can be contacted at noga_a@hotmail.com.

Laura Atkins worked for almost a decade in the children's publishing industry in the United States. She then completed her MA in children's literature at the University of Roehampton in London where she is currently the Conference Manager at the National Centre for Research in Children's Literature. Having done postgraduate research on children's literature and diversity in the publishing industry, she worked with the Arts Council of England to organise a conference with this same focus. Publications include 'Creepy Kids: The Use of the Child's Perspective in Films of the Uncanny,' in *Children's Literature and Childhood in Performance* (2003), and 'A Publisher's Dilemma: The Place of the Child in the Publication of Children's Books' in *New Voices in Children's Literature Criticism* (2004). Her website is www.lauraatkins.com.

Farzad Boobani was born in 1979 in Sanandaj, Iran. He got his B.A. in English Language and Literature from the University of Tabriz, and, having earned the first rank nation-wide in the entrance exam for universities, he started to study for his M.A. in English Literature at the University of Tehran. He graduated with honours in 2003, and he is now teaching English Literature at the University of Guilan, Rasht. His publications include: T*he Ash and the Wind* (a Persian translation of A E Housman's poetry), two short articles on modern Persian poets and a paper on Joyce's *Ulysses* (forthcoming).

Anastasia Economidou is Assistant Professor at the School of Educational Sciences in Pre-School Age of the Democritus University of Thrace, Greece, where she teaches Greek and foreign literature for children. She is the author of *One Thousand and one Subversions: Innovations in Children's Literature* (Athens: Hellenika Grammata, 2000). She currently researches the concept of the implied reader and its ideological function in texts for children as well as the ideological aspects of illustrated books.

Michele Gill is a part-time, final year PhD student at the University of Newcastle- Upon- Tyne, UK. Her thesis examines the representation of boyhoods in contemporary young adult fictions written in the UK, Australia, and the USA. Other areas of research interest include youth culture and Australian Children's Literature. Michele works as the Children's Services Manager for a public library authority in London and teaches modules in children's literature to Childhood Studies undergraduate students at Northumbria University, Newcastle.

Cassie Hague is a PhD student in Political Theory at the University of Exeter. She studies the intersection between politics and literature and focuses on exploring the range of political understandings found in youth fiction. Before arriving in Exeter, she completed an MA in Cultural, Social and Political thought at the University of Victoria, Canada and received her BA from the University of Hull. Her academic interests include political ontology, green theory, feminist theory, ideas of childhood, and the interdisciplinary study of cultural forms. In her spare time, she reads children's novels obsessively.

Zoe Jaques is currently in the final year of her PhD on 'Fantastical Creatures in Children's Literature: 1850-2000' at Anglia Ruskin University, Cambridge. Her research interrogates issues of identity and the environment through evolutionary, post-human and eco-critical theory.

Åse Marie Ommundsen (1972) is a Research Fellow at Department of Linguistics and Scandinavian Studies at University of Oslo, Norway. Her earlier publications include a book on religious magazines for children from 1875 to 1910. Her ongoing research project: *Literature for child or adult? Crossing the borderlines between literature for child and adult*, focuses on new tendencies in Norwegian children's literature. She has a special interest in late modern literature, on which she has lectured and published several articles.

Sarah Park is a doctoral candidate in the Graduate School of Library and Information Science at the University of Illinois at Urbana-Champaign. She received an M.A. in Asian American Studies (2004) and a B.A. in History and Asian American Studies (2002) from the University of California, Los Angeles. Her research interests include the construction of Korean/Korean American children's experiences and identities in children's literature, children's librarianship, social justice, transracial adoption, and Korean American and Asian American history. Sarah critically analyses representations of Korean adoptees in children's literature in her dissertation project. Website: www.sarahpark.com

Alison Pipitone received a Master's Degree in English Literature from Buffalo State College, and a Bachelor's Degree in English Literature from the University of Southern California. Her particular area of interest addresses the implications of cultural, historical, and sociological elements of twentieth century English and American literature.

Jennifer Sattaur is currently a PhD student at the University of Wales, Aberystwyth, researching children's literature and the perceptions of childhood present in Victorian literature from the mid-nineteenth century into the *fin-de-siècle*. Her other research interests include Victorian and *fin-de-siècle* literature, Jungian Archetypes and Eco-Feminist criticism. Recent publications include: 'Harry Potter: A World of Fear', *Journal of Children's Literature Studies* Vol. 3, No. 1 (March, 2006): pp. 1-14; and 'George MacDonald's *Lilith*: Whores in Babyland', Publication Pending in *North Wind: A Journal of George MacDonald Studies*. She is also currently working on a monograph for Pied Piper Publishing entitled *The Trickster in Children's Classics: The Child in the Adult.*

Ulf Schöne's academic background is in Nordic Studies, German Literature and Philosophy at the universities of Bonn, Marburg, Trier and Växjö (Sweden). His Masters thesis was on Tove Jansson's Moomin books, completed in 2000. He is currently a lecturer of German at Stavanger University, Norway. His ongoing Ph.D. project deals with anarchism in children's literature.

Liz Thiel is a lecturer at the National Centre for Research in Children's Literature at Roehampton University where she teaches on undergraduate and MA courses. She has recently completed her doctoral thesis on the family in nineteenth-century children's texts and a monograph based on her research, *The Fantasy of Family: Nineteenth-Century Children's Literature and the Myth of the Domestic Ideal,* is scheduled for publication with Routledge.